WIRED
–FOR–
SUCCESS

PRACTICAL PHILOSOPHIES TO MASTER ENTREPRENEURSHIP & LIVE LIFE ON YOUR TERMS

EDMOND ABRAMYAN

Curious Fortune

LOS ANGELES, CALIFORNIA

Substantive Editor: Suzanne Uchytil
Copy Editor: Kayla Henley
Cover Designer: Hina Khush
Illustrator: Alan Syah
Typesetter: Suzanne Uchytil
Indexer: Onajite Anne Obajuwana
Proofreader: Julie Hart

Library of Congress Control Number: 2021949098
ISBN 978-1-7379521-0-7 (paperback)
ISBN 978-1-7379521-1-4 (hardcover)
ISBN 978-1-7379521-2-1 (eBook)

Curious Fortune Enterprises
8309 Laurel Canyon Blvd Unit 196
Sun Valley, CA 91352
www.curiousfortune.com

PRINTED IN THE UNITED STATES OF AMERICA

The information and advice contained in this book are based upon the research and the personal and professional experiences of the author. They are not intended as a substitute for consulting with a healthcare professional. The publisher and author are not responsible for any adverse effects or consequences resulting from the use of any of the suggestions, preparations, or procedures discussed in this book. All matters pertaining to your physical health should be supervised by a healthcare professional. It is a sign of wisdom, not cowardice, to seek a second or third opinion.

This book is dedicated to those courageous individuals who make the conscious decision to give to the world rather than to take from it— to serve and create for it rather than to just consume from it.

Throughout my adult life, I've given sincere attention to the craft of these artists of life. As a result, I've become fascinated with the potential of the human organism. I must admit, it's through the heroic labors of others that I've found, within myself, the ability to complete this book.

Standing on the shoulders of giants, I have been able to further myself.

Acknowledgments

I'd like to extend my most earnest appreciation to my immediate family. Without this particular family, I would not be who I am today and none of what I do now would have ever been possible.

To my parents—for always providing unconditional love and support, and for giving me the freedom to create my life as I see fit.

And to my brother—for teaching me very early on that all people are equal in their humanness and that I can do anything I put my mind to.

From the depths of my heart, thank you.

I love you.

"Your conflicts, all the difficult things, the problematic situations in your life are not chance or haphazard. They are actually yours. They are specifically yours, designed specifically for you by a part of you that loves you more than anything else. The part of you that loves you more than anything else has created roadblocks to lead you to yourself. You are not going in the right direction unless there is something pricking you in the side, telling you, "Look here! This way!" That part of you loves you so much that it doesn't want you to lose the chance. It will go to extreme measures to wake you up, it will make you suffer greatly if you don't listen. What else can it do? That is its purpose." — A.H. Almaas

---

I would like to highlight and acknowledge the late and great Alan Watts for his contributions to mankind. Through his work, I found a mentor beyond the grave. Though he may be gone in physical form, his efforts will continue to live on, and he will be remembered also through this book.

Additionally, I would like to express my sincere gratitude to all those who contributed to the fruition of this book. There really are too many of you to name but know that this couldn't have happened without you. To all my team, my editors, beta readers, mentors, and friends: Thank you!

CONTENTS

PREFACE

It has become my understanding that self-sufficiency is of the highest importance to the person who aims to live a life of freedom, and self-sufficiency is equally important to the person who aims to contribute any kind of value to society.

Modern culture and education seem to have lost half the meaning of self-sufficiency. Most people only look outside themselves, into their environments, to create self-sufficiency. They hold the belief that self-sufficiency solely revolves around the accumulation of money; they think money will make them self-sufficient and will set them free from their fears, wants, oppressions, and insecurities. This is one of the great myths undermining the common sense of our society today.

This myth creates materialistic views and extreme consumerism within our culture. It causes people to go through life with a lack of meaning, thinking in terms of competition rather than cooperation. People feel compelled to push one step ahead rather than to help pull another person one step forward—unaware that the latter option is the real progress. Individuals go on to plot the courses of their entire lives in accordance with this mentality. As a result, they take positions in life that they have little to no interest in—for the sole purpose of making money.

This modality of thought is completely backwards from what I know self-sufficiency to be. To be a self-sufficient being means to be able to rely on one's self, completely, to create a life of freedom. Freedom from one's own limiting ideas and beliefs. Freedom from inauthenticity to one's innermost self. Freedom to be emotionally and intellectually independent. Freedom to live life and contribute to society in the ways one sees fit. Freedom to honestly express oneself. Freedom to just *be*. The height of self-sufficiency, in my opinion, is that what renowned psychologist Abraham Maslow called *self-actualizing*—what Paramahansa Yogananda, the venerated author, monk, and yogi, called *self-realization*. It's the disidentification of the limited, intellectual sense of self, and it's the drive to realize one's full potential for purposes of self-fulfillment.

Many self-improvement and personal development books have been written on this topic of self-fulfillment. Some from eminent, well-experienced individuals in our society whose accomplishments spread far and wide. Several of these books have gone under the radar, so to speak—missed by those who could have greatly benefited from them. The ones that I've discovered, and the ones in the limelight, have not effectively combined the fields of philosophy and psychology in practical ways that could be operative to an entrepreneur today. And that's where the idea for this book was born—from the realization that the values critical to developing the right understanding of the human organism are directly applicable to the fulfillment of one's hopes and ambitions.

Individuals can indeed realize their deepest desires and capacities and be independently fulfilled. That, however, demands a flexible way of thinking and a certain sensitivity to life. Unfortunately, without the proper guidance, we tend to develop fixed mindsets and rigid worldviews as we grow older and more proficient with our ways. Due to the suffering we experience as a result of this stiffness, we even close our hearts. If, however, we're able to open ourselves up through the perspectives of others, we get to see things a little differently. My objective with this book is not only to supply the reader with useful information, but also to create an environment that helps us see the same things in different ways. This objective will hopefully result in a more fulfilling experience of life lived for those participating—an experience that will ultimately lead people to their own understandings of self-sufficiency.

I chose to write this book not just because I value self-sufficiency, but because I realized I had stumbled upon something quite significant, yet completely ordinary that others have not. Through my accomplishments, I've realized the destruction success can bring upon an individual. Yet, it was through the failures that I learned to develop myself and grow as an expression of life. In this book you will find mindsets, ideologies, and practical techniques that will not only allow you to reach your goals but to experience the satisfaction and fulfillment of living a human life. In each chapter you will be exposed to secrets behind the power of your innate capacities as a human being—secrets that can transform your attitude towards life and propel you into the depths of what it means to live life as this organism.

This book is filled with real-life examples that will help illustrate the philosophies of some of the most compelling individuals to have walked the face of this planet. It will provide proof of mankind's agency to direct the course of their own evolution, and it will also reveal everything one needs to accept their circumstances just as they are. By studying the principles in this book, one will gain an understanding of how they've come to think the way they do and what they can do to align themselves for a future that's more suitable to their desires. The reason behind this book is simple: to expose the consequences of our worldviews and to empower those who want to utilize their potential for something greater than they already are.

Who am I to write such a book? It might seem that anyone who believes that they can write a book on psychology, philosophy, and entrepreneurship must think themselves to be the embodiment of happiness, wisdom, and success; that they have all the answers and everything in their life figured out. This isn't exactly the case though. I'm far from perfect. I've simply realized I cannot lie to myself, and so I continue to learn and grow every day. The arrangement of challenges that have manifested for me to overcome have taught me valuable lessons, and I consider myself quite fortunate for the opportunity.

This book is my best effort to pass some of those lessons on, not from a place above anyone, but from a modest place, where my faults have left valuable memories. This is the path I've chosen for myself though, and it's the path I'm choosing to share with others. It's the path of the warrior, where one aims to overcome themselves regularly. This path, for me, is a work in progress. It's a daily discipline. Ideas and philosophies will change, and I'm open to the growth—as we all should be. However, this book shows these ideas and philosophies as they are now.

In the end, if I accomplish anything, I'd like to provide some food for thought and fuel for change.

Enjoy.

Edmond Abramyan

INTRODUCTION

What would it feel like to know in your mind, in your heart, and in the very depths of your being that you are living the life of your dreams? To know with unquestionable confidence that you're designing your life, as the Supreme Architect would, in the ways *you* want? We all dream of achieving that level of certainty and inner peace, shutting out the noise, and creating life on our terms. We dream of having the independence to do as we wish, when we wish, how we wish. We all dream of being free.

You're reading this book most likely because freedom is what you're interested in, not just money, fame, or riches. People who are solely interested in making money rarely spend their time with books like this. Their minds aren't interested in the *warrior's path*—the slow progression and the accumulation of deep practical knowledge. Likely, they're more concerned about finding shortcuts to a luxurious life, a place where they think they'll finally feel secure and safe within themselves.

Such people are trading their dreams—the things they want to do, the people they want to become—for their comfort zones. From their point of view, real freedom is a hoax, and the only way to "make it" is to have connections to powerful people or to take advantage of others. These people believe that if they have money or power, they won't have to *work* to achieve their dreams. In short, these people often look outside themselves to create change. They think that anyone who has achieved a state of freedom and happiness has come across some massive luck or has traded morality for riches.

They don't understand that humans largely create their own luck.

That may be why you're reading this book—you seek to lift the veil of luck. This book will reveal that freedom and happiness are largely a result of having the right perspectives. It will expound the fact that life is created inside out, and it will give you some tools and points of view to help create further progress in your life.

Take Steve Jobs, Jim Carrey, Andrew Carnegie, and Bruce Lee. What do these individuals have in common? Regardless of your opinion on them and their personalities, these are people who came from practically no wealth and created something so exceptional that generations of people know and will know their names. These four luminaries dived into the immense, mysterious worlds within themselves to bring forth extraordinary lives without. Cultivating their strengths from an awareness of their life experiences, they applied the entrepreneurial mindset (which we will discuss later in this book) and grew to manifest so much.

Consider the life of Bruce Lee. He honed his passions into a discipline and became a famous martial artist, big-time movie star, and revered philosopher; but before all that, he was a juvenile delinquent in a street gang, and he washed dishes and stuffed newspapers for money. One might investigate his past and wonder how his incredible change in fortune took place.

In a letter that twenty-one-year-old Bruce wrote to a friend, he clearly expresses that strict efforts in hard work are just one way to create a good life. Another way is by the use of one's imagination—which requires work too, but also the integration of ideas that haven't been applied before. He stresses the importance of not only originating things, but also of polishing one's abilities and character and of having motives beyond just *making money*.

Bruce was a dreamer, but a practical one. Although he originally owned nothing but a small place in a basement that he rented, he used his imagination to clearly visualize himself overcoming obstacles, learning from setbacks, and achieving his wildest dreams to create a massive five- to six-story Gung Fu institute with divisions all over the States.

After talking about the dynamic (possibly divine) forces within each individual and how one can devote their energy into accomplishing rather than mentally combating themselves, Bruce ends the letter with these lines:

> . . . My will to do springs from the knowledge that I can do. I'm only being natural, for there is no fear or doubt inside my mind. . . . Success comes to those who become success conscious. If you don't aim at an object, how the heck on earth do you think you can get it?[1]

Bruce Lee wasn't the only person curious about the potential of the human being. Before he died, Charles P. Steinmetz, the electrical mastermind who heavily contributed to the expansion of the electric power industry in the United States, was asked the question, "What branch of science would make the most progress in the next twenty-five years?" He shrugged his shoulders, paused, and thought for several minutes, then he replied with complete certainty: "Spiritual realization. When man comes to a conscious vital realization of those great spiritual forces within himself and beings to use those forces in science, in business, and in life, his progress in the future will be unparalleled."

It was drawing on this great transcendent force, this divine spirit within, that turned Bruce Lee from a street hoodlum into a legendary star. It was this same force that turned Andrew Carnegie from a bobbin boy at a cotton factory, earning $1.20 a week, to one of America's wealthiest industrialists and philanthropists. Likewise, Jim Carrey, who came from a financially burdened, once-homeless family, became a famous actor, comedian, writer, and producer. And Steve Jobs, whose birth parents put him up for adoption, became one of the pioneers of the personal computer revolution.

These noteworthy titans understood that the problem is never what you have, who you know, or where you come from. The problem is never who you are, but who you *think* you are (which we will refer to as the *ego*, *self* with a lowercase *s*, or *self-image*). The problem arises when people mistake their psychological thoughts for Truth—when they mistake the stories in their minds for what's happening in actuality.

When people start mistaking thoughts for reality, they go on to believe that external forces of evil are preventing their happiness and wellbeing. In truth, the greatest evil is humankind's own ignorance. In later chapters, we'll see how ignorance—misconceptions about the nature of reality—is the only force that allows suffering to continue in the hearts of humankind.

However, there is a fundamental difference between the way we describe the world and the way the world actually is. People who are aware of what that fundamental difference is are those who have found ways to pause the mental chatter long enough—that is, to pause the thinking, judging, labeling, self-talking. They are among the few who settle into reality.

Christian scholars understand this as the state of mind referred to as "heaven" by Jesus Christ when he said that we should become like little children (Matt. 18:3). It's the state of mind we all had when we were in our youngest years. It's where guilt and anxiety disappear, simply because there's no past to be guilty of and no understanding of a future to be anxious about. Guilt and anxiety are merely ideas, and ideas require thinking. When there's no thought, all that's left is the present moment, the eternal now; and in the eternal now, there is no separation between object and subject, thought and thinker, feeling and feeler. All there is, is awareness—complete, indescribable unity. That is the state of mind of little children before they develop a sense of self.

This is the Truth that many brilliant poets write about, musicians sing about, and thinkers philosophize on. It cannot be put directly into words, because as soon as one attempts to describe it, it's immediately lost. And that's why it's a secret that is right before our eyes.

However, many people don't want the Truth because the Truth can be a difficult thing to hear if we're not in a place to receive it. Most people just want the reassurance that what they know is right;

such reassurance creates a feeling of superiority, even for a brief moment, and pleases the egoic mind.

Many like to hear of these philosophies, sometimes for entertainment and sometimes to simply accumulate information—maybe in order to argue better or to achieve some satisfaction of knowing more than another. This book is not written for those types of individuals. This book is written for people who seek the *experience* of freedom, not just the knowledge of it. To these individuals—the earnest seekers—freedom is in their grasp. However, it comes with a solemn duty, which involves living from the heart and contributing to enhance our communities for true pursuit of the common good.

Let's take a moment to really think about it. What would the world be like if everyone did what they did, but their hearts were involved? At the very least, I think there would be more harmony amongst us and more peace within us. This would contribute to a healthier society with deeper bonds and connections with one another.

This type of society can be built when people employ the purpose of this book, which purpose is that of the true warrior: to make a sincere attempt to understand and apply proven principles in order to grow and overcome—to be better fit to protect, nourish, and contribute.

True warriors are servants to society and to its future. They're committed to a cause greater than themselves. And as committed warriors, they set personal gain aside and act for the greater good.

True warriors defend the defenseless. Their path is one of service. They are always geared and ready to use their talents and abilities to deliver real value to others. They are gentle, yet unwavering, acting with integrity and empathy, and holding themselves accountable for their behavior.

Warriors are dedicated to personal development; they endeavor to improve their daily behavior. They embrace the journey of self-discovery and understand that their only enemy is their own ego. They strive for self-mastery to overcome their personal gratifications and shortcomings. They put their heart into everything they do. They adapt quickly to change and persevere in the face of adversity. They know that life is short and that time is the real treasure, so they value it accordingly.

These are the reasons why the true warrior shows up again and again, regardless of victory or defeat.

Every human being has this warrior spirit within them—in this book, we'll call this the (higher) *Self*—it's our highest ideal brought into fruition. It reveals itself with the subtle but unmistakable urge to grow and reach new heights. Its energy is expressed as a desire to experience something more, to feel something greater.

However, people don't always apply this energy. Often people give in to their ego, or their past conditioning, and use their warrior energy for personal gratification, in ways that ultimately hurt themselves, those around them, and society as a whole. Other times, people sell themselves short to please others; consequently, they choose paths inauthentic to their heart's desires. These people don't live an analyzed life. It's a sad ordeal when people waste their abilities on things that, in the end, don't really matter to them.

To remedy the nightmare of wasted talent, this book will uncover not only your potential, but also the mysteries of how people create lives on their terms, unapologetically, from the inside out. Utter bliss. Complete joy and satisfaction. Perfect harmony and a sense of ease. These are what freedom feels like; and it's available to you the moment you let go of all the things weighing you down.

Equipped with the information and practices in this book, you, the earnest seeker, can be one of the few to understand what you're capable of. You can find your direction and begin creating the life of your dreams. You can find your freedom and align yourself for a self-sufficient lifestyle.

It all starts by looking within and getting to know your Self.

Let's begin.

No human being is
an exception to the
human condition.

THE HUMAN CONDITION

Nan-in, a Japanese master during the Meiji era, received a university professor who came to inquire about Zen.

Nan-in served tea. He poured his visitor's cup full, then kept on pouring. The professor watched the tea overflow until he no longer could restrain himself. "It is overfull. No more will go in!"

"Like this cup," Nan-in said, "you are full of your own opinions and speculations. How can I show you Zen unless you first empty your cup?"[2]

Going Under

Just before turning twenty-seven, I was given one of the greatest gifts hidden within an unfortunate event.

Friday morning on September 29, 2017, I was laying on a gurney in a hospital gown, being rolled into the operating room. The last thing I remember about that moment is the surgeon making a remark about how I was one of the few patients he'd ever seen cheerful about a surgery *before* getting the anesthesia.

How else should have I been? I looked forward to having my body repaired and being back on the mats. Little did I know at the time, I was in for quite an experience ahead.

It was two days later, the evening of Monday, October 2nd of 2017, a day before my 27th birthday, when things really started to click. It was dark. I was sitting upright in bed with my legs extended in front of me, a pillow behind me and another under my arm, trying to fall asleep. I couldn't slide down and lay completely on my back because I felt immense pain the moment my body went completely horizontal. This was an intense four-and-a-half-hour-long shoulder surgery; one that was going to take time to bounce back from.

About a year and two months prior to this day I experienced a bad fall while competing at an international Brazilian jujitsu tournament. As a result, I tore the cartilage in my shoulder socket that held the ball of my joint in place (the labrum). With my judgment clouded by adrenaline and a sheer determination to finish the fight, I continued and injured myself further.

It sounds bad, and it was. But the physical discomfort was nothing compared to the conflict going on in my mind that night.

My thoughts were racing, and I couldn't stop or slow them down. The thing is, I wasn't thinking about the pain in my shoulder or the taxing operation I had just gone through. Instead, I was thinking about how my life got to where it was and what I was going to do going forward.

On paper, things looked great. I had built a successful company from the ground up that allowed me the opportunity to take care of my bills and help my disabled parents even more. I now had better choices, more variety, and additional conveniences that I didn't have before. Best of all, it gave me the freedom to work completely on my terms. I was no longer living paycheck to paycheck. For a young man growing up in a family on the lower end of the socio-economic hierarchy, this was a big deal. I went from waking up to a loud, annoying alarm only to deal with corporate politics to rising and sleeping when I wanted, working with whom I wanted, how I wanted, and for the most part, when I wanted. I was enjoying fancy dinners, spending time with people I enjoyed, taking extended vacations in foreign countries, and training martial arts in the afternoon while everyone else was at work. I worked hard to get to this level, and so I was doing all the things I thought I wanted to do.

However, beneath the surface, unbeknownst to those around me, there was a great deal more going on with me. Over the course of the previous several years, I had been experiencing severe bouts of existential dread—there was a profound sense of meaninglessness that I just couldn't shake. I completely changed my life's path, and in the process developed a great deal as an individual, but the truth is, as grateful as I was for the lifestyle reaching a few of my business goals allowed me, the satisfaction was short lived. I learned the hard way, tying your happiness to a goal is a surefire way to end up depressed. "I'll be happy when…" never works the way you think it will. If you don't reach your goal, you're upset; if you do, you're joyful for a moment, then you become upset again and want more.

I understood that being a business owner, no matter how successful, wasn't going to fill that inner void. And now that I couldn't train anymore, it felt like another part of my identity was falling apart. With no sense of clear direction, I felt hopeless inside. If someone were to probe my mind, all they would come across at the time was uncertainty. Life didn't make much sense, but it was obvious that more money wasn't going to solve this problem.

It wasn't until later that I understood I had experienced a massive shift in values from the growth and new lifestyle. It turns out developing a deeper perception of life and my place in it tossed me into a state of mind where I began to question my belief systems, ways of life, identity, and really, reality itself.

There was a clear disconnect between me and my personal power. I built an incredible business but somewhere along the way I lost track of the creation process. It's like I had effectively forgotten how to be confident in my abilities. I found great difficulty putting trust in myself for the things I wanted. This is what happens when you make yourself out to be a victim in life.

Really, life happens for you, not to you. But it's hard to accept that and show up for yourself when you're looking from such low places; all you see is misfortune, because that's all you're looking for.

And, that's really where I was—in a low place. My body language expressed it, too. My arm was in a sling and I was always hunched over with my shoulders in, chin down, and eyes mostly to the floor. Emotionally I was drained and the once positive and optimistic attitude I had seemed to have faded away.

I heard somewhere that businesses are merely reflections of their owners. I found that there's profound truth to that. I created my business so that I could have more freedom, more flexibility, and more joy. However, throughout this period of my life, it was more like a set of chains—like I had created my own personal prison, and it was slowly exhausting me.

Over time, my finances began to reflect that, and so did my relationships. At that time, I regularly felt misunderstood. My parents relied on me, and I felt like I was failing them. When one area of your life is frustrating you, and you don't confront it, it begins to seep into other areas and cause disorder there too. I realized that how you do one thing is generally how you do all things.

Looking back, there was a real fear of taking ownership of my life and committing to what I really wanted for myself. This manifested as doubt, indecision, and behaviors of looking outside myself for approval. I had this idea of me as a busy person, doing important things. Except, I was without purpose, worrying and working harder than I should have on things that didn't matter as much to me. What I really wanted seemed way out of reach, so I never truly dedicated myself. Even though I was no stranger to accomplishment, part of me didn't feel capable or deserving. I was also already comfortable with my new lifestyle, and I didn't want it to change so soon. But now because of this injury, I was given the painful opportunity to confront everything.

It felt incredibly lonely, and all I could remember at the time was being anxious about my future. I didn't know whom I could trust or what I could do to bounce back and regain my confidence. My friends at the time didn't understand the path I was on, and my immigrant parents barely spoke the English language, let alone recognized what I was trying to do with my life. It looked like I was alone and destined for failure. The excitement about my recovery process had vanished and I was left feeling miserable and unsure of myself. It was awful.

What could I do though? I thought to myself. It was late in the evening, it hurt to move, and I was tired from the all-day-long mental sparring match I had with myself.

I decided to just sit with it all.

My room was quiet and all I could hear was the sound of an occasional car passing by through my open window. There was a slight breeze that brushed up against my foot that was sticking out from under my blanket. It was then that I began to realize, once again, on a more profound level, that I have myself to live with for the rest of my life; no one was coming to save me. I had to learn to take care of myself, for myself—in all aspects of life. I made the decision to accept my situation and let go of the idea of an immediate or even quick recovery. It was going to take some time until I regained my strength, and I became okay with that. I told myself I would just do what I could when I could, then I would do a little more next time. And if I needed to rest, I would rest—no unnecessary pressure. One day at a time. If this was my cross to carry, so to speak, I would carry it without complaint, just on my own pace. Feelings of peace began to settle in.

Shortly after accepting the physical pain as part of the process, the itch to do something dropped and it was like a load off my shoulders had been lifted. As I continued to breathe, I realized this gripping sensation within begin to slowly release, and then suddenly, I realized a distinct separation between myself and my own thoughts. It felt strange at first. It was like I was behind a field in which thoughts were happening, and from there, I was looking forward and watching them pass by. One by one, they came and went. I had read about "observing your thoughts" like this in the past, but it was the first time I remember experiencing the sensation of being the *watcher*. The best analogy I have come up with thus far is that it was like how the outer layers of an onion falls off. I understood how

I was identifying with an aspect of me that could so easily be peeled away. My idea of myself was just that, an idea.

My mind became empty, and I was in a completely open and receptive state. Thoughts would arise like before, but this time, because I had this *place* I could go—this fresh reference point as *the observer*—I was able to dwell in the stillness a little longer each time before becoming attached to another thought again.

This brought to mind a question worthy of entertaining: If I'm this thing—separate from my thoughts—that's watching my thoughts, what part of me is it that's aware of me watching my thoughts? In other words, who's observing the observer, who observes himself watching over his own thoughts. And how far back did this go? How many *observers* are there? And which one am *I* really?

What happened next was a simple yet boundless and complete experience, not meant to be understood with the intellectual mind; only because, well, as soon as one starts to think of it, it's concealed with the veil of thoughts.

Herein lies the human condition and the problem of the limitations of language.

The Limitations of Language

Saying this at the start of a book is ironic: *words can sometimes be a real hindrance.* Just by inspecting the nature of words and our use of them can we realize their clear limitations.

Words are mere symbols, used to represent and communicate abstract ideas. We use these symbols in the same way our great ancestors did on the cave walls—to help others visualize particular things or events. The words we use today are simply enhanced versions of these wall paintings. We've grown, and so have the things we've seen, created, and experienced. Thus, as our species has advanced, so have our symbols.

We see this evolution in common language today. For instance, when we create or discover something new to us, we need something to call it, so we assign it a word. Then we use other words to define

our new word. Thus, our words are made up of collections of other words; or, put differently, the only way to express a word's meaning is to use other words. These labels of things upon labels of things (which labels we call "language") give us a rudimentary but nonetheless powerful form of communication.

However, these words can only take us so far.

Bruce Lee expressed this understanding of the limitation of words in his movie *Enter the Dragon*, when the character he plays strikes a student upside the head for stopping to think after Bruce's character asks how the student felt about his practice. In the scene, Bruce's character emphasizes feeling over thinking while he methodically uses his finger to point up at the moon, conveying that if his student were to concentrate too much on the finger, the student would "miss all the heavenly glory."[3]

From watching this brief scene, we see that Bruce understands the distinctions between symbol and reality, and he understands that humankind often confuses one with the other.

This dilemma likely stems from our species' early development, from the time when we first discovered and used symbols on rocks and cave walls. Throughout our species' evolution we have found symbols to be so unbelievably useful to our survival and advancement that we have become completely immersed. As a result, we too often blur the lines between reality and our mental concepts.

No human being is an exception to the human condition. We can sometimes forget or, more commonly, overlook the fact that we are undergoing the experience of being what we've labeled a *human*. We can sometimes forget that we're enduring life with a human mind in a human body, interpreting the world with a human super-computer-brain—all of which are things that we know very little about.

Surely our instinct to inspect and to label has brought us a long way in our intellectual understanding, but in the end, how can we dare make a claim that we *know* anything when our intellect and reasoning is ultimately bound by our limited five senses?

We have words to recognize and describe incredible forces like space, time, gravity, heartbeats, and our breathing, but we really don't know a thing about what they *are*—yes, we know what these words mean intuitively, but none of us can actually rationalize and explain their existences. How do we know what we're labeling as *empty space* isn't actually some substance we can't interpret with our five senses? In relation to this disconnection, many scientists go so far as to claim that our experience of reality is just a bunch of hallucinations we collectively agree upon.[4]

Thinking we know what these physical things are is like thinking we know the taste of a fruit just because it's been described to us. However, this is how society has trained us to view ourselves and our experience of life.

The Connected Universe

Concentrating primarily on the faculties of intelligence (memory and reason), our Western culture's philosophy has influenced a viewpoint that humans are separate, isolated beings, living disharmoniously with the world and needing to confront and control that world just to survive.

What if this isn't the case at all? What if our own intellect and reason obscure the truth of our existence? What if, on the most basic levels, we do have a deep connection to the universe, to nature, and to one another?

Consider that the common view of the Earth being a big rock floating in space—covered with separate, distinct, living organisms—isn't the only view of reality that a person can think up. Let's entertain this approach: The earth is to the solar system as organs are to an organism. So just as the skin grows hairs and the trees grow leaves, the earth grows people. Within this worldview, our existence on this planet would be an expression of the solar system and its balance, just as much as the solar system is an expression of our galaxy and its balance.

What prohibits us from this view is the issue that has existed throughout recorded time: the belief that we are separate from one another and the universe—the lack of awareness that we are one and the same. We all have connections behind the curtains of our intellectual understanding, running far deeper than our imaginations can fathom.

We can explore these underlying agreements between *self* and *environment* through deep meditative practices, concentrated breathwork, or psychoactive agents, or by experiencing an altered state of consciousness labeled a mystical experience or cosmic consciousness. When undergoing this transcendent experience, we can realize that either everything that's happening is our own doing, or we realize the exact opposite of that: we aren't doing anything, and all our decisions and actions are happenings of nature.

Describing either of these seemingly opposing viewpoints is describing the same thing: we experience our own activity and the activity of the goings-on in nature as one single process—the complete coming-together of the transactions between environment and organism.

The Patterns of Thought

When we look throughout recorded history, we see all types of men and women, regardless of position and social class, encountering the same existential problems and feeling the same feelings we do today. Topics such as meaning, purpose, spirituality, and empowerment have been contemplated for ages. Although time has brought us to an era of incredible luxury and extraordinary tools, each person's fundamental, inner experience of life remains unchanged from one another.

Unfortunately, we now live in a culture where it's viewed as more "normal" to take a one-in-fourteen-million chance at winning the lottery than to invest just ten to fifteen minutes a day into ourselves—enriching our thoughts and experience of life. Statistics show that Americans today spend an average of seventy billion dollars per year on lottery tickets[5] and only twenty-six billion dollars on books.[6] Our society believes that money can solve all problems and that the lack of it is the source of all problems. Society also believes that one must be born rich, encounter some incredible luck, or commit wrongful acts to become materially wealthy. Yet statistics show that over eighty percent of millionaires are self-made by legitimate means.

Thankfully, we have the lottery winner to prove otherwise—they almost always seem to end up right back where they started shortly after cashing the big check.[7]

Now, I'm not claiming that money or lottery tickets are the problem, nor am I arguing that books are the answer. Rather, I intend to direct attention toward our patterns of thinking: how our beliefs build our destiny, and how we falsely believe that we can change our experience of reality solely by changing our outer circumstances and our surroundings—solely by accumulating more money.

Although our environment is obviously a major factor in our experience of reality, little of our experience relies on what's actually *out there*. Instead, the conditions of our experience have more to do with the meanings we assign to them, and those meanings say more about what's going on inside us than about what's going on outside us. In simpler terms, what we think and feel is happening overrules what's actually happening. We see this principle play out in the example of the twin brothers who were raised by an alcoholic father. One twin became an alcoholic; when asked how he got to where he was, he responded, "I watched my father." The other twin never touched a drink while growing up, and when he was asked the same question, he gave the same response: "I watched my father."[8]

Here we have a simple model showing how individuals' perspectives on life's circumstances influence their everyday common sense. Likewise, this model helps to show that much more than life is lived inside out and that our problems lie not in our circumstances but in the paradigms of our thoughts.

The Universal Self

We don't generally view our lives as part of a process nor feel any sense of connection to the world outside our skin. Instead, we usually identify with only an idea of our self, the ego. We become an individual person, a somebody, and we go on with our lives, unconscious of this fact, playing the roles that come with the serious character we've decided to adopt. And since most of us are trained to believe we are what we are called, we begin completely identifying with these roles. Then we chase the many desires that come with each role, the regular cravings of the ego: approval, attention, status, recognition, position, power, control, and so on.

These desires rooted in the ego aren't necessarily bad, but they aren't necessarily good either. The requirements of the ego are endless; they'll never truly be satisfied. Trying to satisfy the ego would be like decorating our own prisons, trapping ourselves in our own minds, and drowning ourselves in our own thoughts. At the same time, we can't escape the ego's requirements; they are a natural part in the processes of life. What matters, then, is to transform our attitudes to embody a more practical view, one that ultimately serves us.

We're not just the roles we go on playing in our day-to-day lives. That much should be clear. Our idea of our self is only as much of us that we can fit into our conscious attention in any particular moment. Our idea of our self doesn't include any information on the unconscious, biological marvels of our existence—the ways our organs and blood flows work, the ways we use our muscles, the ways we breathe, the ways we interpret energy flowing in nature, or the ways we actually experience consciousness altogether.

The idea we have of ourselves in the Western world—the idea of the ego—is incomplete. Looking at it through an Eastern philosophical lens, we're actually something far greater.

For example, in Hindu tradition, the universe is the theater of God; from this point of view, God is not some old, wise, long-bearded man in the sky. God is the Self behind the self. This Self is the One who repeatedly births itself into existence to put on these masks and assume these various roles. Why? Merely for the purpose of exploring and entertaining itself. Life with this worldview is a huge drama—or comedy—where a person could approach all things sincerely but without attachment. From this position, life's not such a serious thing.

We can learn to see life in the same way. We each have this responsibility to break the bondage of our brains' processes and shatter the illusions of the ill-prepared mind. By living from a lower and simpler place, where self reflects upon Self, we take the careful journey through the visible and sensory world and into the intelligible world. Here we become *the observer*—watching and eventually accepting the conditioned mind and its endless pursuits. Maybe then we can recognize the self that struggles as the grand illusion itself, as shown through a line from *The Matrix*: "There is no spoon, Neo."[9]

With this recognition in mind, the age-old query of "Who am I?" can be brought into a different light with this suggestion: the true Self is the entire universe arranged and centered upon our entire being, conscious and unconscious, as well as upon our surrounding environments. The real Self isn't exclusive to our body and its mechanisms but is something far greater, and that's why we can't intellectually understand this.

The Other and You

About 13.8 billion years ago, the Self was the big bang, and as time went on it developed into human beings—you and me—who then lost track of their original nature. In other words, we are the entire universe experiencing itself at the place we call *here and now*. The things we do are also the doings of the environment we're in. The creator is observing itself through us. As Alan Watts—a brilliant writer and a champion of Buddhism, Taoism, and Hinduism—would say, "Your behavior is its behavior, as much as its behavior is your behavior. It's mutual. We could say it is transactional."[10] One doesn't have any actual power over the other. They act in unison. It's like driving a car and using a steering wheel; when you're trying to make a turn, you pull one side of the wheel down, and as soon as you do that, the other side goes up. The up and down are synchronized; there's an underlying agreement between up and down, just like with an organism and its environment.

An age-old adage says, "You can't know yourself without knowing about the other."

The only way we're able to define ourselves is by our relationships to the other; we know who we are in terms of our environment and of other people. "I'm this thing *here*, and you're that thing *there*. I'm tall and you're short; you're fat and I'm skinny; I think this way, you think that way. If it weren't for you, I wouldn't be me; if it weren't for me, you wouldn't be you." It's like leaning two playing cards on each other when trying to build a tower of cards—they each stand up because they support each other. If you were to take one card away, the other would fall. They interdepend, just like we do.

We're not separate, isolated beings. We're all backs and fronts to each other. We and our environments are all interdependent systems, coming together to form the One entire system—the universe.

We didn't come into this world from some other place; we grew out of it, just like the plants, birds, mountains, and everything else. We grew out of the world the same way a wave grows out of the ocean—both separate from and a part of the ocean, the wave grows, rises, then collapses into itself. Human beings everywhere are like distinct waves, manifesting themselves as *you* and *me*, and giving us each the individual experience of *I*. And although we may be separate and distinct waves, we still have the same ocean deep within us. We are of the same source.

Forgetting our source and identifying solely with things such as race, ways of life, faith, color, or profession—aspects of the ego—inevitably splits us apart. Furthermore, when we identify entirely on these shallow levels, we create in our minds a worldview that adds to our feelings of separateness and creates an unnecessary tension between and within ourselves. Then the problems we face become ours alone, as if we're the only ones who have ever encountered such adversities.

Except, the reality is that there isn't one problem someone can face today that hasn't been faced and conquered by someone before. No one is isolated in person, problems, or experiences—we are all connected and part of the original Self.

The Awareness of Self

Even though our environments and capabilities differ from person to person, the fundamental experiences of human life don't. And although we may experience different circumstances and situations, we all feel and experience consciousness in the same ways. We all share this experience of existence in a similar type of physical structure, with a similar type of mental makeup and emotional nature. Our fundamental experience of life will always remain the same as one another.

Those people who coined the term "know thyself" weren't only directing attention toward our personal preferences, habits, and desires; they were also referencing something far deeper. Learning to observe how the world and its systems operate and how we relate to those systems can be significant to our development as human beings. Bringing together the outer material world—what was once a playground for us as children—with the inner world of thoughts and feelings can meaningfully propel our growth by revealing deep insights into our own psyche—into our souls. From this position, we can begin to see *how things happen*, we can begin to know God.

Given the magnificent and unique self-aware capabilities of human beings, our nature requires us to learn, adapt, grow, and create.

The only problem with these magnificent abilities is one that has plagued mankind since recorded history—the problem of confusing what's in our mind for reality. Thankfully, in this day and age, we have many examples of *I*'s well lived, or *waves* well waved. As we open ourselves up through their examples, we'll discover many antidotes to the general conflicts we face in our lives.

Maybe if we open ourselves up in that way, we will find it—the paradox of enlightenment. The way to find our Self by losing our self.

The tao that can be told is not the eternal Tao. The name that can be named is not the eternal Name.

The unnamable is the eternally real. Naming is the origin of all particular things.

Free from desire, you realize the mystery. Caught in desire, you see only the manifestations.

Yet mystery and manifestations arise from the same source. This source is called darkness.

Darkness within darkness. The gateway to all understanding.

—Tao Te Ching, *Lao Tzu*, verse 1

"Even now, at this very moment, what our brains are doing for us is miraculous.

2 THE ILLUSION OF REALITY

A man went to a Buddhist monastery for a silent retreat. After he finished, he felt better, calmer, stronger, but something was missing. The teacher said he could talk to one of the monks before he left.

The man thought for a while, then asked: "How do you find peace?"

The monk said: "I say yes. To everything that happens, I say yes."

When the man returned home, he was enlightened.[11]

The Musical Universe

The universe is not like a business. There's absolutely no need for the universe to fulfill anything. It has no goals or objectives of its own. Its existence is essentially playful, and as such, it's best understood by analogy with music or dance. The purpose of music and dance as art forms is lively expression. We say one *plays* the guitar; they don't *work* it. The idea is the same with dance. A dancer never aims at a precise location on the dance floor because that's where they *should be*. The whole point of dancing is the dance itself.

In this sense, music and dance are different from travel—the analogy that's impressed upon us in modern times. When you travel with fixed plans, your aim is more serious; you're trying to get somewhere, and you generally want to get there as fast as possible. That's not the point with music and dance. The end of the song or dance isn't the goal. The goal is to be fully immersed in each note, in each step, in each moment. The goal is dynamic expression.

This is the same awareness that the entrepreneur represents, and it's what sets him or her apart from the businessperson. Entrepreneurs are pioneers, they take complete ownership of their lives and carve out their own path. Businesspeople are more like administrators; they follow systems and procedures and try to get the most out of what they can with what they have. The entrepreneur is the innovator; he or she works *on* the business to deliver value to others, whereas the businessperson is more of a manager and works *in* the business, focused on the bottom line. Although the entrepreneur is thought of as having some future vision in mind, much like the artist, he or she understands that there is no real end point, no finish line—the painting is never completely done, just like the vision can always be improved upon. The businessperson is results-focused and works with tangible qualities that can be measured. The entrepreneur, however, just wants to create things; he or she is sincerely—not seriously—involved in the process for the sake of being involved in the process. The businessperson plays the finite game, where there the intent is to beat the competition—to win. For the entrepreneur, it's an infinite game where the objective is simply to continue playing—much like life itself, much like the universe itself.

This isn't something our modern education system helps to instill in us though. Instead, we have a method which produces an entirely different influence on our thinking. Everything is either right or wrong; and that's determined by someone else, often regarded as an authority. What we've done is created a hierarchical grade system that entices a young child to *join the system* and *stick with it* until this thing called "graduation." The child is put into first grade and given the impression that it's not enough to be there; they must move on to second grade, and then from second grade to third, and so on. Then, when they finally finish their grade school, they move on to middle school, and then high school. Things begin to accelerate; the now-teenagers are now being *prepared* for the coming graduation.

Once that's out of the way, if the system has caught the individuals' interest enough, the young adults start all over in college as freshmen and work toward another graduation in yet another establishment labeled "a school for higher education."

Then, finally, when they're done with their higher education and have entered the so-called real world, they join some other organization with a hierarchical system working toward this new thing—another warped idea of "success" that's heavily influenced by others.

"Work hard. Meet that deadline. Keep at it! That *great thing* is coming. It's just about here!"

Then, they wake up one day, middle-aged, at an executive-level position. They think to themselves, "I'm here!" And they don't feel any different from what they've always felt.

Alan Watts concludes this idea:

> Look at the people who live to retire, to put those savings away. And then, when they're sixty-five they don't have any energy left; they're more or less impotent. And they go and rot in some senior citizens community. We simply cheated ourselves the whole way down the line. We thought of life by analogy of a journey, with a pilgrimage, which had a serious purpose at the end. And the thing was to get to that end. Success, or whatever it is; or, maybe heaven after you're dead. But we missed the point the whole way along. It was a musical thing, and you were supposed to sing, or to dance, while the music was being played.[12]

The rest of this chapter will describe how the human being falls victim to this destination-driven concept of life, and what's required in order to return to harmony.

The Senses and Symbols

Thanks to modern science, we know that the entire universe, including this world and the walking miracles that are you and I, is made of patterns of energy vibrating at different frequencies. We humans interpret these energy patterns using our own built-in tools and supercomputer-brains. Even now, at this very moment, what our brains are doing for us is miraculous. Our brains decode the sounds, visuals, smells, tastes, and physical sensations as bits of data from the vibrational world we're a part of. When we engage the world of energy with our eyes, ears, nose, tongue, and skin; we allow ourselves to interpret the world into things we call light, noises, scents, flavors, and textures. As our brains process the information they receive through our sense organs, we experience what we call thoughts and feelings. By processing a wealth of energy patterns, like solving immense mathematical formulas, our brain is giving us—bags of skin and bone—the sensations of life.

To be accurate, sounds and sights don't exist anywhere "out there." The only way sights, sounds, tastes, smells, and sensations can exist is if there's someone or something nearby that is equipped with adequate tools to distinguish them. We experience the senses within us, through our interpretive tools. Tastes need mouths to exist; light needs eyes. The question about the tree falling in the forest and making a sound—it's just energy patterns vibrating through the air; if there's no one there to hear it, there's no sound.

Just as sounds and sights are merely signals in our brains, our thoughts and emotions are literal neural signals with a makeup of complex, mathematical patterns. It's the same with memories: although they affect the way we perceive the world, recollections are moving bits of data, still being processed, floating around in our brains. We interpret the data as the past, but just as there's no such thing as the future, there is no past. Everything in our experience is in the present moment—the process of mathematics being solved by our brains.

I'm not implying that nothing exists in reality—just no *thing*. A *thing* is a symbol; it's a word we made up for purposes of speech. Words aren't a part of nature. They are a part of communication, and *communication* is an idea that we invented—just like *time* and *money*. But in nature there are no separate things; there is just One, and the unfolding of One. Calling anything a *thing* is labeling it as

something distinct and separate; that's the source that our illusions stem from.

Consider this: we call it an "illusion" when we experience a distortion of our senses. For example, an artist's painting of an optical illusion and a ventriloquist's ability to speak through a dummy are illusions caused by our internal systems. The illusions are characterized by perceptions that appear different from the version of reality we're used to; our senses reveal to us what we'd like to see, what we think we should see. These illusions are based on the general assumptions the brain has made, given the information it has accumulated and what it believes is happening. Put another way, we've learned to place so much significance on our own ability to think—on our memory and our rational mind—that we believe the illusions to be Truth.

Illusions can also be related to the habit of excessive thinking—thinking so much that we confuse reality with abstract symbols such as words, numbers, images, and ideas. When we confuse reality with symbols, the very things we use to capture, measure, and understand reality take the place of reality itself. Like when an individual has an unwavering preference for money over tangible consumable wealth. Or, as Alan Watts puts it, when someone confuses the clock for time, thinking, "The sun rises because it's six in the morning."[13]

In this paradigm of thinking, man can salivate over the menu in place of the meal, give his attention to computer applications in a screen rather than the people around him, and even prefer digital pornography in place of real-life intimate interactions. Another example, one increasingly relevant in today's culture, is when a person photographs a remarkable moment just to show and talk to others about it on social media; surprisingly, some people seem to have even more fun online than at the event where the photo was taken.

When Common Sense Media surveyed around a thousand participants in 2018 through their research program, their results found that nearly half (44%) of the participants felt frustrated with their friends for being on their devices while they were hanging out together. An even greater percentage (54%) admitted to becoming distracted by social media when they should have been paying more attention to the people they were with.[14]

All these examples emerge from the misfortune of confusing what's in our minds with the truth of what's really happening; the misfortune of growing more self-centered and disconnected from reality.

The Habit of Excessive Thinking

Expressed as simply as possible, thoughts themselves conceal Truth. And this isn't a new plague. About 2,400 years ago, Plato wrote the Socratic Dialogue, *Republic*. In it, Socrates describes the "Allegory of the Cave." Like a poet describing the indescribable, Plato used the magic of words to illustrate the ways we fall to the habit of excessive thinking.

In the "Allegory of the Cave," Plato describes a group of people who have been chained inside a cave, facing a blank wall for all of their lives. The only things they can see are shadows projected onto the wall in front of them from figures passing a fire behind them. These shadow puppets have become reality for the group. Even after being told about the world outside the cave, most of these people continue to believe that the shadows are all that exists. The members of the group who wonder about the outside world are in the worst turmoil; they are fixed in speculation, and they are also hesitant to break free and leave what is familiar. According to Socrates, these shadows are the closest these people get to reality.

This allegory expresses the state of civilization sometime between 380 and 360 BCE. However, many of us are still chained in our own caves today. The shadows are an analogy of our thoughts. The world of thinking is all that some of us know. We allow words, calculations, examinations, worries, frustrations, signs, and symbols to be continuously flowing through our consciousness, so much so that we've begun to identify with them; we've begun to think that we are our thoughts.

This type of connection to our thoughts causes us to view life in terms of strict effort and correct action. The attitude is always, "We need to think the best thoughts, have the best ideas, and execute the best methods in order to get to that place where our version of *things* will be better." To a person with this mindset, nothing else matters, mostly because there's no awareness of anything else mattering. The individual is operating completely from the intellect and is bound by the limits of the analytical mind. The signs have become everything, and the destinations those signs are taking the individual to are all that's important.

René Descartes, who is often referred to as the father of Western philosophy, is famous for the phrase "I think, therefore I am." He clearly displays the error of Western society's thinking with a full-scale identification of the shadows on the wall of Plato's cave. Further, it gives insight as to why people in the United States are said to be the most depressed people in the world.[15]

Thinking is an incredible power, but it is not who we are. The intellectual mind allows us to cut, dissect, and analyze. It gives us the ability to remember, to plan and coordinate, to communicate, and even to identify. Furthermore, it gives us the capacity to *know* that we know, establishing knowledge and setting us apart from the rest of the animals. However, even with all these brilliant abilities, this power of thinking is just one of our capacities; and it is not the most profound one.

Most people recognize that knowledge differs from wisdom. Knowledge gives us a way of looking at the universe but doesn't help us see it for what it actually is. Knowledge gives us a story about the universe—and a fascinating one at that—but ultimately this story is just words. Collect a thousand words and we have a picture. Yet even with the ability to hold ten thousand pictures in each of our minds, we're still no better than what we see before us. Thus, we recognize our essential need for wisdom. Without wisdom balancing our knowledge, we're lost in the illusion of the stories we tell ourselves in our minds.

When we believe that these recycled stories are Truth, it's natural to feel different and isolated from everyone else, to feel stuck in our heads. Our perspectives are tuned out from what's really happening in nature. When this happens, how can we intuitively recognize the harmony behind everything? The magnificent dance is just a huge purposeless movement, and the music echoes nothing but a racket.

When we aren't tuned in to the playful rhythm of life, we're all swimming upstream; slowly but surely, our mind's flexibility atrophies. We lose our ability to see life the way it is. Consequently, we see ourselves as something more and more separate from what's around us. Eventually, a self-centered point of view takes over, and we're powerless to conduct ourselves efficiently—we become distracted and create a serious problem out of *nothing*.

At this stage of the habit of excessive thinking, a person's situation resembles that of a substance addict. The illusive signs they crave provide a temporary rush; after every hit the individual feels at home and on track. With rationalization after rationalization, the person goes on, suffering the dark night of the soul. Lost in concepts of who they think they are, what they think they need, and what they believe they should do, they remain stagnant, with limited perspectives of their true nature. Hence, they look outside themselves for the inside-answers they sincerely yearn for.

However, if the individual can cultivate a deeper sense of self-awareness, this state of inverted awareness doesn't last for too long. As we become more self-aware, although we're able to fool our minds with our rationalizations, deep down beyond our minds' sensory interpretations lies the understanding that deception is taking place.

What should a person in this position do? What is the wisdom that balances a mind that is heavy with knowledge?

The answer is simple—"I don't know." Because when we're in such a position, our task isn't to do anything. "I know" entices us to do the things we know; knowledge leads to action, and action is not what we need in this situation.

Instead of action, we need wisdom—being. Our task is to find a way out of the thinking mind, out of identifying with memory. Wisdom isn't simply believing the information we've collected. True wisdom is directly seeing and understanding for ourselves. The point is to carefully examine facts that contradict our beliefs, instead of just accepting the first or most emotional piece of information that is offered to us. Then, from there, to be open to changing our beliefs to counter the inflexible and intolerant parts of our nature. Like a sculptor, we must slowly carve out the excesses of our perspectives, discarding the viewpoints that no longer serve our wellbeing, growth, and fulfilment in life. This is a step toward healing from our past and achieving peace of mind. This is how we realize our human potential. This is how we become wise.

The Call to Self

There can be no wisdom without the pure heart-mind connection that establishes a pathway for intuition to flow. Consequently, there can be no knowledge of *the way* of the universe—what Eastern Asians call the "Tao"; what Hindus call "Brahman"; what Christians call "God."

The process of opening this channel and allowing the inflow and outpouring of *the way* is incredibly simple, but it's no easy task to accomplish. People can't pick themselves up by their own feet; or, as some say, "pull themselves up by their bootstraps." Just by trying, a person would waste an incredible amount of energy. We're better off accepting that we'll never improve ourselves or the world. We are the way we are, and things are just the way they are.

One might wonder, "But what about this ceaseless urge to improve?"

We shouldn't try to improve ourselves, strictly because the part of us that is trying to improve ourselves is the same part that needs improvement. Adopting the perspective that we can't improve ourselves by strict and rigid effort frees the energy we need to allow a higher aspect of ourselves to intervene. It's precisely during this process of *not* trying to improve ourselves that we find ourselves on a path toward improvement. As the great cosmetic surgeon and author Maxwell Maltz once said, "Accept yourself as you are. Otherwise you will never see opportunity. You will not feel free to move toward it; you will feel you are not deserving."

The only way in which we can be sure that we aren't hindering our improvement is if we stop trying so desperately to improve. This involves the temporary suspension of any judgement of one's current and past self and the removal of any results-seeking type of behavior. Instead, we should find aspects of our lives to be grateful for, and at the same time use our imaginations to see ourselves as already being the type of people we want to be. From there, with playful aims to find our own beat, the right action will come about on its own, and our only duty will be to act on the impulse and keep the momentum going strictly for the sake of keeping the momentum going. With this approach, the *work* starts in the mind and reverberates throughout the body and soul.

The Rhythm of Life

Life and entrepreneurship are musical things—a dance. In a dance, if you make a mistake, you don't stop and start over, nor do you go back. You continue forward as best you can, and by the time the step comes around again, if you have managed to keep up with the patterns and the beat, you'll be ready to perform correctly.

The idea the professional dancer carries from one movement to the next is the idea of surrender. Surrender in this context doesn't carry the same weight as the surrender a warrior would experience submitting in war and giving themselves up as a prisoner to their adversary. Rather, it's like the surrender one experiences giving up their breath to an exhale—to allow for an inhale. It's surrendering something old—the burdens of the past—to make room for something new. In this sense, the grip on how things are and *should be* becomes released, and the weight is lifted. From this framework, the dancer is loose, unrestricted, accepting, and trusting, allowing the music to carry them from one motion to the next.

Like the dancer, if we maintain an open mind that accepts all of life's conditions, our perspectives naturally become pliable. And if a sincere desire is there, we will find our way. Otherwise we'll continue on unwaveringly, seeing life in the same ways, experiencing the same types of problems, wasting opportunities, and failing to mature to play higher parts in the glorious unfoldment of nature. In the case of the latter scenario, the unused potential would be equivalent to a bird choosing to walk on its feet, never seeing the world from the sky.

People don't deliberately decide to cheat themselves out of their own lives though. Most of the time, it happens unknowingly because they're so deeply entrenched in the material aspects of life—to the chatter in their minds—that they don't know of any other way to be (like those chained in Plato's "Allegory of the Cave"). As a result, they don't believe there's anything better, that they deserve any better. Concentrating so much on the forces operating outside themselves, they're unaware of their own powers of self-sufficiency—they're unaware that they're wired for success. They can't see their own wings, their own potential, so they can't feel truly, independently fulfilled.

Sadly, even with directions at their feet, most people won't choose *being* over *doing*, mainly because people do what others do. However, to the person turning inward for freedom, conformity is the most elaborate prison—conformity twists will into habit, depletes courage to the point of complete submission, and prevents the individual from experiencing the freedom that is within reach.

There's a requirement to turn inward and become increasingly aware of ourselves entirely—thoughts, feelings, and all. That's where we drop our obsessive desire for material fortunes to uncover and shed the layers of conditioning that is negatively affecting our beliefs of the universe and of our places within it.

When we direct our attention to the internal world to understanding the Self—*the way*—our perspectives can naturally adjust to realize what many great people before us have realized: our true nature—our actual fortune.

"I am; therefore, I think."

Like a brush that covers
a canvas with paint, our
thoughts shape our reality
through our perspectives.

3 THE FILTERS OF PERCEPTION

Three friends took a road trip together.

While cruising through a city, all three friends were rather quiet with one another, busy thinking within themselves.

The driver was thinking about his upcoming promotion and was rationalizing buying a newer, more efficient vehicle.

The passenger to his right woke up late and didn't have time to make himself breakfast; he was a bit hungry and was wondering when his friends would be too.

The friend in the back had recently broken up with his girlfriend and was optimistic about finding a new partner.

After a while, when they had completely passed through the city, they began talking amongst themselves.

The driver said, "That town must be filled with a lot of rich people. Did you see the nice cars everyone drove?"

The passenger to the right said, "I don't know about the cars, but they sure had a lot of nice restaurants; people there must struggle to choose a place to eat."

Then, the friend in the back, "Why don't we spend the night? Didn't you see all the beautiful women in that town? Let's go back!"

Filtering Our Realities

The universe is boundless, and the happenings within it are infinite. There's certainly more than meets the eye at any particular moment, in any particular place.

Most of us have already recognized that our human senses are limited. There are certain frequencies of thought (including sensory input) that we just can't access regularly in our current state. We've never seen radio waves or heard a dog-whistle, yet we have evidence of their existence.

What about the things we have access to, though? What about the things within our scope of sensible reality?

The story of the three friends on a road trip illustrates that our experiences of reality are shaped by our outlook and focus; our thoughts directly influence our experiences.

In the previous chapter we discussed how the entire universe is information—a bunch of ones and zeros waiting to be decoded. Our brains take this information and convert it into experiences that make sense to us—sensations, scents, savors, sights, and sounds. There's an abundance of information for our senses to interpret at any given moment; however, our brains can only process so much of it at any given time without breaking down.

To keep the brain from overloading, a network of neurons called the *reticular activating system* (RAS) facilitates the overall level of consciousness and acts as a filter. In the subconscious levels, the RAS determines which vibrations of energy to let through for us to experience. At the same time, it's also making sure our brain doesn't have to deal with more information than it can physically handle.[16] We can relate it to a camera lens that only captures the specific area it's aimed at.

A great example of the RAS in action is a person's ability to hear his or her name called even in a noisy environment. Another example is when someone desires a particular type of car and then starts to notice more of that type of car around. The more we think about something, the more we subconsciously look for it—even to a point where we'll convince ourselves we've found it even though we really haven't.

The RAS acts as our personal secretary, letting in only the things it believes to be important for us. And the things it believes to be important are the things we ourselves believe to be important—our deepest beliefs and the things we focus our attention on the most.

This is how some entrepreneurs seem to find themselves exactly at the right place in the right time with the right information. By keeping a question or problem in mind long enough, without a gripping attachment to any answer, the brain is bound to naturally begin looking for the best solution. One could be standing in line at the post office and overhear a conversation which just so happens to spark a reference in their mind. Their RAS was primed and deeply tuned to pick up the frequencies which communicated their breakthrough. So often, this deep mental work of creating a vision and aligning beliefs and focus is mistaken as the mysterious force of luck.

All human brains work this way. There is the conscious part, which is the thinking or "self-talking" part; and there's the subconscious part, the body, which is like a deep memory bank that we call on for information. The conscious part is our awareness in the present moment, and it inputs data into the subconscious to help us simplify the navigation of life. For instance, anyone who can walk has had to learn which muscles to use to make walking happen. Through consistent, repetitive practice, we program the act of walking into our subconscious minds. Then, throughout most of our lives, we usually don't need to put strenuous effort into walking; we have all the necessary data already within us.

Although this input (programming) is most effective in children,[17] it happens with any information that the brain accepts— information the reticular activating system lets through. And that's information that already fits within an existing belief system: information that we're interested in, or information that can pose as a threat to our survival. All other information is discarded or opposed. In this way the brain continues to ensure we're always getting what we deeply want out of life.

Consequently, our experiences of life are merely a result of our interpretations—of what we choose to accept. The way in which we frame life's circumstances programs our minds to certain points of view. Because of this, even though the world behaves in a limited number of ways, we each have an incredibly unique experience of life.

We are the artists, our thought is the paint, our minds control the brushes, and the resulting paintings are the realities that our perspectives shape. Like a brush that covers a canvas with paint, our thoughts shape our reality through our perspectives.

Choosing Our Perspectives

Just a simple switch in perspective can create a completely different reality for an individual. This can be leveraged by interpreting each situation as a challenge presented to us to learn and grow from; or we can interpret each situation as either a blessing or punishment. The former interpretation develops into a valuable inner discipline, while the latter inevitably leads one to the victim mentality—"this happened to me."

A "this happened to me" individual thinks about whom to blame for situations; an individual who takes complete responsibility, though, automatically thinks of possible solutions to problems. The first person asks, "Why did this happen to me?" The other asks, "Is this in my power to fix? And if so, how can I fix it?"

The victim mentality perspective will never empower anyone, let alone create opportunities for personal growth. It puts the focus on the outside world and completely keeps a person at the level where he or she is frantically reacting to life's circumstances rather than calmly and appropriately responding—being the effect of life's outcomes, rather than the cause of redirections. However, an inner-disciplined individual has the habit of taking complete responsibility, complete ownership.

Cultivating the inner-disciplined approach will put the individual in the driver's seat of life. Instead of only looking for opportunities, the individual will create them. The hope of "build it and they will come" will be replaced with the faith of "I'll find a way; or, I'll learn to find a way." For example, an inner-disciplined individual who's looking to enter the marketplace won't wait for customers to show up—he or she will find ways to get in front of and attract the ideal type of client. Because inner-disciplined individuals take the initiative, they have a wider variety of life experiences.

This radical difference in one's quality of life is possible because just a slight adjustment in perspective transforms challenges into catalysts for strength and deeper experiences. This change of perspective can also mold us into more sensitive, vulnerable, and gentle beings, allowing us to have deeper connections with others.

When we really think about the significance of perspective, we realize the incredible power in assigning meaning to our circumstances and begin to recognize how we're truly wired for success.

In *Man's Search for Meaning*, Viktor Frankl, an Auschwitz survivor and neurologist-psychiatrist, discusses the necessity of having meaning in life. As Frankl writes about the horrifying experiences of the Nazi concentration camps' inmates, he shows that the inmates who believed that there was definite meaning in the suffering they experienced were the ones who went on to survive the ordeal. On the other hand, individuals who were unable to assign any significant meaning to the torment found themselves helpless and hopeless; consequently, they gave up on life and died in the camps.

Most people don't realize that they can assign their own unique meanings to their life experiences; they don't know that they don't have to take circumstances at face value. Sure, Viktor Frankl was imprisoned in a concentration camp; but instead of viewing the entire situation as mere torture, which view would have led him to believe that he would die a horrible death there, he chose to believe that although this was an incredibly horrific and painful experience, his time in the concentration camp would later benefit him and all the lives he touched.

It can be startling at first to recognize exactly how much responsibility we have over our own mindsets, directions in life, and sense of freedom. The realization can throw us into a state of panic or even constant hesitation. Holding ourselves accountable can be frightening because when we give ourselves the authority to assign our own meaning, we simultaneously create the possibility in our minds that we will choose to see things the "wrong" way.

It's like when we hold off on making an important decision. If an individual hasn't spent much time cultivating an inner-discipline, and as a result feels disempowered in their lives, they're likely to become stuck or feel paralyzed in the face of a seemingly important decision; they're afraid to make the wrong choice. They may rationalize needing more information, even when they already know enough to make a choice. As a result, they hold themselves back, sometimes never deciding at all—letting life decide for them. Having this in mind, it may benefit an individual to see that although there is a right choice, there is no wrong one.

Understanding Life in Contrasts

Human consciousness distinguishes by contrasts. This is because the inner goings-on of the brain—which interprets our experiences—work with an elaborate organization of *on*s and *off*s. The various neurons in our nervous system either fire or don't fire; in other words, our awareness is completely made up of an enormously complicated arrangement of yeses and nos. It's just like how a video camera or television system works—recording and displaying in pulses. It's also the same principle that lies behind our computer systems and all other electronic innovations. These technological systems and the workings of our brain all come down to a matter of *zero* or *one; no* or *yes; off* or *on.*

Contrasting elements must exist in order for us to understand the world. Consider the idea of *height*—we understand height by the words *tall* and *short*, establishing our opinion of each based on the other. The thought of *tall* isn't really understood without comparing it to *short; short* doesn't exist until there is something tall. You can't completely separate *tall* and *short*—just like you can't have good without bad, right without wrong. One actually implies the other.

Each side is a part of the same process or the same concept. *Left* is to *right* as *up* is to *down* and *back* is to *front; background* and *foreground, noise* and *silence, empty space* and *filled space;* these opposites arise simultaneously. We need one to understand the other.

In East Asian philosophy, this idea is expressed well through the yin-yang symbol. Two opposing parts—one of black with a white dot, and one of white with a black dot—come together to form the symbol. Scanning from top to bottom, we see that some parts of the symbol have more white, others have more black. But when we look at the symbol as a whole, we see how perfectly balanced everything actually is. That's why the symbol is called "yin-yang," not "yin and yang." These two identical yet opposite halves cannot exist without one another.

Naturally, we want to experience the "positives" (pleasure, good, light, life) and avoid the "negatives" (pain, evil, dark, death). However, we need to let go of the idea that we can capture more white and avoid black—more good and less bad. That type of mindset falls along the same lines as looking at a fence from only one side; eventually, we begin to deny the idea that a view from the other side is even possible.

There will be more about this in future chapters, but for now it's important to realize that it's impossible to clearly and accurately judge the true nature of a given circumstance. The truth is that from the human standpoint everything in nature is relative and seems dualistic. There's nothing that is good or bad in reality; however, *thinking* something is good or bad makes it so. The popular and effective psychological treatment practiced by thousands of therapists worldwide, cognitive behavioral therapy, is based upon this very idea. When people can abstain from making judgements, especially negative ones, about their daily life situations, they can liberate themselves from a great deal of needless suffering. Even Epictetus, a renowned Greek Stoic philosopher, agreed and said, "Men are disturbed, not by things, but by the principles and notions which they form concerning things."

By accepting the idea that good and bad are just recycled thoughts and that we mentally create and interpret our experiences of life, we can open the door to the perspective that life is happening *for* us, not *to* us.

"The world as we have created it is a process of our thinking. It cannot be changed without changing our thinking." —Albert Einstein

Human beings always
follow through with who
they believe they are.

4 THE SELF'S MENTAL BLUEPRINT

When Bankei held his seclusion-weeks of meditation, pupils from many parts of Japan came to attend. During one of these gatherings a pupil was caught stealing. The matter was reported to Bankei with the request that the culprit be expelled. Bankei ignored the case.

Later the pupil was caught in a similar act, and again Bankei disregarded the matter. This angered the other pupils, who drew up a petition asking for the dismissal of the thief, stating that otherwise they would leave in a body.

When Bankei had read the petition, he called everyone before him. "You are wise brothers," he told them. "You know what is right and what is not right. You may go somewhere else to study if you wish, but this poor brother does not even know right from wrong. Who will teach him if I do not? I am going to keep him here even if all the rest of you leave."

A torrent of tears cleansed the face of the brother who had stolen. All desire to steal had vanished.[18]

The Need for Variety

Let's picture ourselves walking through a forest, from one side to the other. We would notice many different plants and animals. Directing our focus to the trees, we'd probably identify pines, redwoods, cedars, and so on. They're all trees, but they would differ from each other. Each would have a unique set of characteristics.

Now let's picture ourselves looking closer at each individual type—say, to the redwood trees. We'd find that each redwood still differs from every other redwood. Some would be taller, some thicker, some angled one way, others growing another way. Throughout the entire forest, we'd never find one redwood tree completely identical to another. This is part of what makes forests such a beautiful phenomenon in nature.

Walking through a forest and seeing the same exact tree over and over throughout the trek would make for an unbearably dull experience. After a few yards, one would probably start ignoring the trees altogether, only paying enough attention to not walk into one.

For the forest to be a forest, it needs variety. In the same way, humans need some surprise, some uncertainty, and some unfamiliarity; that need is biologically and psychologically hardwired into us.[19] There's an essential need for different types of human beings on the planet, just as there's an essential need for different types of trees in a forest.

Under the billions of stars live the billions of members of the human family, and they are all at least a little different from each other. *Tall, short, big, small, dark-skinned, light-skinned.* Like trees, we each grow with varying characteristics, all of which are necessary for the development of humankind. *Smart, strong, selfless, kind, courageous, patient, witty, warm, friendly*—all these varying characteristics develop from an individual's personality and intelligence, which are two contributing factors to how a person deals with the world and the people in it.

Although we're not equal in our abilities, we're still all equal as human beings, and we have more in common than otherwise. We all love, fear, learn, feel pain, feel joy, feel anger, and so on. We all want to have a greater experience of life, and we all want the least amount of suffering as possible. Our commonalities are important, as are our differences. Our commonalities keep us together, and our differences keep us interesting and help us creatively evolve.

The Power of Self-Image

This understanding about the development of our personalities and intelligence points to something in psychology called the *self-image*.

Dr. Maxwell Maltz categorized the self-image as "the most important psychological discovery of this century."[20] He claimed that our characters and behaviors are directly linked to the ways in which we see ourselves—our understanding of our individuality. His research shows us how our mental blueprints of ourselves (our thoughts about ourselves) have a straight connection to our habits; if our understanding of ourselves were to change, so would our habits.

A great analogy that expresses the idea of the self-image is a room that is set to a certain temperature with a thermostat. Say the room is set to sixty-five degrees. If you want to raise the room temperature to seventy-five, you can't just turn on the stoves and fireplace, use a space heater, or invite more people into the room to make it warmer. Eventually, the thermostat would activate and the room would adjust back down to sixty-five degrees. No matter what you do, you cannot keep the room's temperature at anything other than sixty-five degrees for too long before the air conditioning unit kicks in and the temperature readjusts. You must change the thermostat itself to get a stable adjustment.

Our character and behaviors work the same way. We cannot force changes in our behavior and continue to look at ourselves in the same way. If we want lasting changes, we must alter the ways in which we see ourselves—our internal dialogs about our self—together with our habits. This process takes imaginative efforts since much of our ideas of our self is programmed before the age of seven. For this reason, psychologists place an important emphasis on improving our perspectives of our upbringing and other major events in our lives—our story.

To illustrate the importance of how significant our views about ourselves are, we can take as an example the way some elephants are trained for the circus. (I'd like to stress that this type of training is abusive and not condoned by any means. It is merely used as an

analogy to help the reader better understand the point that's being made.) When the elephant is just a baby, its leg is chained to a stick that is dug into the dirt to keep the stick in place. Throughout its adolescent years, the elephant tries to pull itself free. Because it's just a baby, it doesn't have enough strength to break the chain or pull the stick out from the dirt. It can't set itself free no matter how much it tries.

One might think, "What about when the elephant grows and has the strength? Surely, it would be ridiculous to force a giant elephant to stay in its place with a stick in the dirt."

That's where it gets interesting. From a young age, the elephant's mind is conditioned to think that the chain has a hold so strong that it will never be free. And so the elephant carries this way of thinking all the way through its adult years; even when it is grown and has more than enough strength, the mental conditioning is so strong that the elephant never even tries to break free. The elephant doesn't have the self-awareness to recognize its own conditioning. Thus, it stays victim to its habituation and sets its limitations according to its past.[21]

Brutal, right?

Unfortunately, we're not so different from the elephant in this situation. More often than not, we're confident that certain things are or aren't for us. With enough repetition and mental conditioning, we become so accustomed to the ways in which we navigate life that we don't even stop to consider other, possibly more effective ways of thinking, being, feeling, etc. Similar to putting on the same shoe first every time, we're prone to thinking in the same ways every time. Continuing onward like this, we leave ourselves vulnerable to becoming rigid in our views and further reinforcing the self-image we've become familiar with—the identity we've attached ourselves to. Even if we break free momentarily by the strength of will, self-sabotage mechanisms kick into gear, and we go right back to where we were. This is because the self-image's influence in the subconscious mind will always overpower conscious decisions and will.

Like a continuous cycle, results from previous experiences shape identity, which then shapes future experiences and results. This cycle happens because our views, capabilities, and behaviors all stem from the people we believe ourselves to be. Then, we respond accordingly to further reinforce that self-image within our minds. Simply put, the ways we think about ourselves are the chief causes of our personalities, attitudes, and behaviors. The life-circumstances we place ourselves in, the things we think we like, the activities we entertain ourselves with, the disciplines and hobbies we practice, our conduct in our relationships—they all develop according to the thoughts we hold about ourselves.

Human beings always follow through with who they believe they are. The compassionate people are always first to provide aid and support; the empathetic to understand rather than judge. The individuals with the victim mentality will always find a way to put themselves in a situation where they can blame others. The people with the chips on their shoulders will consistently attract conflict and create tension. Our self-images are so deeply fixed into our thought patterns that we will very rarely do anything that compromises the identities we've each established for ourselves. All our actions, feelings, behaviors, abilities, and potential become consistent with those mental images we hold of ourselves. For example, the people who see themselves as smokers and habitually call themselves smokers will be just that—smokers. We each have a powerful psychological urge to remain consistent with how we define ourselves; it's that urge—not nicotine, not any other chemical—that prohibits change.

We're each chained to an invisible stick in the dirt, conditioned by our own ideas about ourselves and about how reality works. The chains are our patterns of recycled thoughts, telling us who we are, what we believe, what we're capable of, and where our places are in this world. Thankfully, we're also the ones who can break those chains and set ourselves free. As Lao Tzu said, "When I let go of what I am, I become what I might be."

The Limits of Self-Image

"I know myself."
"That's who I am."
"That's just the way things will always be."
"This is just how my life is."
"It's my luck, my fate."

These are all manifestations of a rigid mind—a hindrance to the ever-present and ever-evolving forces within us that are operating to help us grow and get what we want from life. They sprout from deep-seeded beliefs of unworthiness, as if we're undeserving of our true desires. By emotionally clinging to these restrictive thoughts, we needlessly get in our own way, adding further roadblocks in between where we are and what we really want.

We live as the people we believe we are; we stay congruent with the identities we've appointed for ourselves. When our ambitions are beyond what we believe is possible for us, we mentally rationalize avoiding them; our true desires remain unfulfilled. In these circumstances, we don't try for what we want because we're afraid to fail, afraid to experience the pain of the unknown, afraid to have people dislike and not respect us for what we're doing. We fear the voice that, when disappointment arises, whispers in our heads, "I told you so. You couldn't do it—once again."

We can observe our thoughts to know our strengths and weaknesses, and that will certainly help us excel in our endeavors; but this paradigm of observation will only take us so far since these are qualities about us that change through experience, worldviews, and the lapse of time.

With observation, patterns in our thoughts can reveal aspects of our self-image; but it's in the empty spaces in between those thoughts that we can truly get to know the higher order of ourselves—the warrior within.

Eventually, we appreciate the fact that our self-image is incomplete. We realize that for us to truly know ourselves would be like tasting our own tongues or looking into our own eyes without a mirror. As Alan Watts puts it, "The godhead is never an object of its own knowledge. Just as a knife doesn't cut itself, fire doesn't burn itself, light doesn't illumine itself; it's always an endless mystery to itself."[22]

We can never completely know ourselves because we're in a constant state of progress—like a flowing river. We may recognize a river by its geographical location when we see it, but because it's continuously flowing, it's never the same body of water twice—it's never the same river we see. Just like this, each of us is never the same person two days in a row—or even two minutes in a row. Each experience and memory adds to our beings. When we sleep in the evening and wake up the next day, we've gained the experience and understanding of yesterday, and it contributes to our beings today; even on the most subtle levels, it has changed us.

These ever-moving and ever-changing forces exist within us even on a biological level. Our physical bodies are constantly renewing themselves. During every second of our existence, the atoms within us are coming and going. We completely renew our entire physical makeup every seven to ten years on average. We have new stomach linings and intestines every five days. Our skin renews itself once every two to four weeks. The red blood cells in our system come and go every four months while white blood cells live more than a year. Within ten years, we have a completely new skeletal system. Our bodies are amazingly dynamic fields of energy and information, ever flowing and ever renewing.

With this perspective, the only thing that keeps us stuck living the same experiences of life is our *self*—our ego—the memories and ideas we have and the meanings we've decided to attach ourselves to. Rhythms and patterns are all they are. Our principal duty is to merely become aware of the rhythms and patterns. It's in this awareness that we can discover the energies to produce change.

"What is necessary to change a person is to change his awareness of himself." —Abraham Maslow

At the core of our
understanding should
be the realization that
we are our own centers
of experience.

5 BEING SELF-AWARE

Two men were arguing about a flag fluttering in the wind.

"It's the wind that is really moving," said the first one.

"No, it is the flag that is moving," contended the second.

A Zen master walked past and overheard the debate. He said, "Neither the flag nor the wind is moving. It is mind that moves."[23]

Seeing the Patterns

1, 1, 2, 3, 5, 8, 13, 21 . . .

The Fibonacci sequence—a fractal; a self-replicating pattern that's able to sustain itself with itself and appears the same at different levels. As the pattern grows into higher stages, it transcends and includes the level before it. This is how the sequence develops.

Patterns are clear and consistent throughout nature. The formation of flower petals, pinecones, shells, hurricanes, human bodies, the Milky Way galaxy, and so much more—they all form and grow within the same model with mathematical precision.

Consider the smallest level—an atom; a nucleus with orbiting electrons.

On a larger level, consider the Earth; it has an orbiting moon. Now, even bigger—our solar system; a sun with orbiting planets.

Looking closely at everything large and small, we can see that absolutely nothing is out of place; not even by 0.01%. We need the plants, the plants need us; the flowers need bees, bees need flowers. If something were only slightly out of place, things wouldn't be. *We* wouldn't be.

These patterns create order and dismiss the idea that everything is random and chaotic. That's why we learn about these patterns in our schools. If we can begin to understand a pattern on its smallest levels, in the microcosm, we can also begin to understand it on its largest levels, the macrocosm—as above, so below.

However, the present school curriculum does not teach about the vast internal world that exists within each of us and the unmistakable patterns we can find there. That's why people should never go to school in search of purpose for their lives—that's found within. Each person has his or her own unique personality and variety of interests. One thing that will bring satisfaction to a certain individual might not completely gratify another. Modern public schooling doesn't encourage this inner exploration though; instead, it encourages the child to fit into a mold and to do what others are doing. This is the opposite of introspection and self-expression.

Just as marvels in the world around us operate systematically, we ourselves have patterns that we've adopted to best fit our survival and growth. The trouble is that behaviors that were once used for our benefit, or even survival, can later keep us from a better quality of life. And therein lies the importance of becoming more mindful of these patterns.

If a sculptor never notices a rough edge, the sculptor can never begin to smoothen it. Like the master sculptor, the more we're observant of our own natures, the greater our chance for emerging out from the conditioning we've molded ourselves into. By understanding the connectivity and interdependence in the world's patterns and our own involvement in those patterns, we become familiar with the goings-on behind the curtain.

Because the course of our lives is dynamic and is in a constant state of change, becoming self-aware can be an uncomfortable and

frightening process at times. Journeys inward to understand who we are as human beings on the deepest levels can be unpredictable. They force us to question ourselves intensely—our intentions, our views, and the stream of our thoughts. They spark curiosity to think deeper about the decisions we make and the true reasoning behind our beliefs and desires. And while we do so, they grant us a deeper awareness of our self and the lives we lead. Most importantly, these journeys give us a realization: the best friend we have is also our worst enemy—our self.

Seeing the Reflection

If it's not taught at home or at the institutions established to educate us, critical information about our true nature becomes overlooked; consequently, an individual's imagination can deteriorate to that which is set forth by society and cultural norms. It's understandable, though; the way in which we've formed our systems and the way in which we handle the upbringing of children don't exactly pave a road toward understanding the value of self-awareness or the ever-present interdependence between us. We're just not there yet; at least, not in our Western communities and homes.

Just observe how before a child is even born, the parents, aunts, uncles, siblings, and many others are already deciding who the child will be. The father may imagine his child someday practicing law. The mother may look forward to teaching the child how to play the piano. An uncle may be excited to bring the child into the kids' martial arts class. Often, these are people who innocently believe they know what's best for the child's life. Consequently, before religion, schooling, and society get their opportunities, the child is already trained—consciously or even unconsciously—to undertake the role of a piano-playing attorney who knows how to throw a punch.

We human beings are born completely dependent on our parents and caregivers for survival. Throughout our childhood, in order to feel safe knowing that we will be taken care of and that we belong and are loved, we mold our behavior into what we believe is expected of us; we emotionally bond with our caretakers in whatever ways available to us. In doing so, we pick up various beliefs, perceptions, and judgements on such things as how to love, how to get approval, how to relate to others, how to meet our needs, what roles to play, and even what life is about. Regardless of how much our parents and caregivers love us, they're by no means perfect; they themselves went through their own patterns of learned behavior from their parents. Consequently, along with the wholesome bonding experiences, they also offer some that are counterproductive.

Patterns of behaviors we picked up in our early childhood tend to carry on into adulthood; and we can notice how the counterproductive ones end up working against us as adults. These patterns include the way we think about ourselves, our conduct in relationships with others, and how we adapt to various types of situations.

For example, a child who has experienced a sense of abandonment or has had overly controlling parents may grow to develop people-pleasing behaviors. Or a child with an overly protective parent might grow to have a disagreeable personality and more rebellious tendencies. Those who have experienced neglect, abuse, or trauma may automatically assume blame, disregard their own needs, and harmfully attach to anyone who shows interest. There will be more on this in a later chapter, but for now it's important to note that these self-esteem issues tend to make people feel unworthy or incapable of leading their own lives. People in this condition are inclined to look outside themselves to be told what's right for them.

In our modern culture, the difficulty is that even though we're naturally self-aware beings, we're not exactly encouraged to question our own thoughts and beliefs. While growing, instead of being moved to inquire and search for answers ourselves, many times we were just told how things are. Because of this, many of us grow to become experts on how to accumulate and memorize information, but not on how to think, and not on how to really understand. And because of the pressure we feel with the passing of time and the expectations of others, it's common to feel lost, stuck, or unfulfilled—as if there's a particular thing we must do or have.

At the core of our understanding should be the realization that we are our own centers of experience. We dance through life and into death in our own shoes. Our comfort should be in knowing that deep inside, there's a symphony playing to guide our steps, and it yearns to be heard. Its only pain is that few of us can stay quiet long enough to listen. Hence, there's no better person to turn to in order to chart the direction of our lives than ourselves.

We can either take ownership of our situations and direct the course of our lives, or we play the passive role—the "this happened to me" role.

The feeling most of us have allowed ourselves to be trained into is the feeling of being completely separate from life around us, and that makes it easy to think that things happen *to* us. At its foundation, this way of thinking is an insecurity about our source, our roots.

These insecurities turn a person from being a valued contributor to an idle, self-centered consumer—we can see this clear in the personalities of our economic giants who've mastered business but not themselves. Careers become nothing more than a means of exploitation and an avenue for profit; the person's gain is more important than the value they aim to deliver. Applying effort in areas that mean little to nothing for us builds the foundation for a meaningless life—and it happens because we direct the course of our lives according to someone else's idea.

This pattern is ours to break.

Is this the example we want to pass down to our children?

Identifying the Outside Noise

Reflect on how many unknown Beethovens we have who exist as miserable doctors, or how many Pasteurs exist as mediocre musicians who have genuine compassion for the healing arts. Picassos as lawyers; Shakespeares as businesspeople. Could there be another Nikola Tesla among us, working a life-leeching job, concerned more about his finances than about cultivating a curiosity for the universe and its workings? And all this because these individuals' ideas of success were shaped by others.

It may be upsetting, at first, to think how those we hold close and respect dearly could be such hindrances to our lives—but it's not just them. It's not just the expectations and opinions of those closest to us that are keeping us from reaching our potential. There's also a constant bombardment of noise all around.

For instance, there are people who earn millions simply by capturing our attention and sharing their messages with us, trying to influence the way we think and see ourselves and others, and with no concern about positive or negative consequences. Tobacco companies are notorious for this. In the 1940s, they hired doctors and dentists to endorse their products to lessen public health concerns about smoking risks. In the 1950s and 60s, they used celebrity endorsements. And in the 1990s, they implemented kid-friendly cartoon characters to appeal to the younger generations.[24] In 1991 alone, the tobacco industry spent $4.6 billion—more than $12.6 million a day, $8,750 a minute—on advertising and promoting cigarette consumption.[25] Their efforts led to an incredible amount of people picking up the dangerous habit. Situations like this happen because the average person doesn't understand the subconscious effects of these advertisements and how they're carefully designed to attack the weakest parts of the ego. Appealing to our pleasures, filling our minds with doubts about ourselves, and adding to our feelings of separateness, these messages easily and discreetly make us feel inferior. Then they pitch their solutions—their products and ideas.

This isn't just in business or politics; it's everyone, everything—knowingly and unknowingly participating in this occurrence. Because we're connected with everything around us, we're always influencing everything, just as everything is always influencing us, whether we're aware of it or not. Concepts on what we should do, how we should live, what we need; what's right or wrong, good or bad, fun or boring, for us or not for us; these are all recycled thoughts in society. The more people accept a certain thought, the more chance there is of that thought becoming the social or cultural norm.

Just like how we program a computer by storing information and creating rules, functions, and limitations, we program ourselves with the information we choose to entertain and accept. In this sense, our minds are like computers—calculating, computing, and working with information given to them. Osmosis—we unconsciously operate in the ways demonstrated to us.

The old saying, "Tell me who your friends are, and I'll tell you who you are," isn't far from the truth. On the shallowest levels, one might hear this and look to their acquaintances; and though it's true that like attracts like and that there are similar mindsets among individuals who spend lots of time together, there's far more depth to this adage than is immediately visible. In this case, our "friends" aren't just the people we choose to spend time with. Not only is there a gradual assimilation of ideas, beliefs, and behaviors among people, but research shows that literally everything in our scope of experience influences our minds—the colors, images, and decorations we see; the text we read, the shows we watch, the music we listen to, the scents we smell. Everyone and everything are constantly influencing our minds and shaping our thoughts; it's just that we're not consciously aware of this process—especially without the practice of reflection.

Recognizing the Influences

We're operating on more levels than we can be consciously aware of, and there are many different processes at work, putting together the lives we experience and understand. The more we think about it, the more we realize that the things we've collectively learned to recognize as "normal" are just patterns of thoughts we've accepted and chosen to hang on to—such as thinking we're a separate, distinct individual, independent to the life happening around us. These are just the stories that we learned to repeatedly tell ourselves.

We owe it to our innermost Self to learn to recognize the various influences shaping and shifting how we see the world—how we interpret the massive transaction taking place between *this* environment and *this* organism. The only reason we're even alive is because this transaction continues to take place. If one is ever curious about the innermost workings of this transaction, they can begin to study their breath and the exchange in between nature (environment) and organism.

By having an experiential understanding of this transaction, and not just an intellectual one, we can understand the significance of what it means to be this particular being—not based on the artificial viewpoints we've adopted from society but based on Truth.

Only when we're away from all the noise can we pierce through the constant racket of desires, pleasures, and complaints—and through our illusion of control. Then, perspectives can become renewed and chaos can return to harmony.

We are ever-evolving, self-transcending beings. By bringing together the inner world of thoughts and emotions with the outer world of sensory experience, the patterns become clearer and we know *the way*.

Be still. Listen.

The cost of not following the heart is spending the rest of eternity wishing we had.

The Man who ceaselessly looks to uncover Truth, finds his Self.

He finds Freedom.

Our psychological states depend on the perspectives we have about ourselves and about the world around us.

6 THE SELF THAT LEADS ITSELF

"Knowing others is intelligence; knowing yourself is true wisdom. Mastering others is strength; mastering yourself is true power. If you realize that you have enough, you are truly rich."

—Tao Te Ching, *Lao Tzu, verse 33*

The Flow of Nature

Which of these two phrases more accurately represents your way of thinking?

The universe helps me. It wants me to learn, grow, and have a joyful experience of life.

The universe is against me. It's a dog eat dog world. You can't trust anyone.

If the previous chapters have successfully expressed any point, it's that our perspectives determine our overall behavior. The worldviews we entertain directly affect our methods of dealing with our environment, both in order and in chaos—life's so-called obstacles.

The course of our lives may not come with maps and step-by-step directions, but we're all guaranteed some twists and turns. If we approach every situation in our lives with the idea that circumstances are to benefit us in some way or form, we direct our mind to work completely differently than if we were to believe that any force is against us. Believing that things happen *for* us adjusts our reticular activating system and prompts our natural intelligence to find solutions to those things we label "problems." When we can reflect on our conditions with our emotions aside, we allow for an unbiased examination; we can see our options clearly. In this non-attached state, we have access to a point of view where reason and imagination aren't clouded.

This method of reflection reliably sets one up to "bounce back" from adversity, right onto a path toward inevitable growth—where challenges are viewed not as forces to resist but as opportunities for personal development, inner development.

For example, we can look at one of the major turning points of Steve Jobs's life to see how chaos was turned into great opportunity. In 1985, Jobs was fired from the world-changing company he founded, Apple. In his words, "What had been the focus of my entire adult life was gone, and it was devastating—I was a very public failure." This left Jobs feeling humiliated, ashamed, and defeated, with thoughts of running away. The company that he spent countless sleepless nights slaving away in a garage for, building from the ground up, was stripped away. Without a doubt, his life was thrown into a state of chaos, with much uncertainty. A situation such as this could bring anyone much grief. However, Jobs didn't allow himself to stay down too long. He realized that although he was outed from his own company, he still loved what he did. The fact that he was no longer a part of Apple didn't change his creative passion. According to him, it actually liberated him and launched him into the most creative period of his life. Over the next five years, he started two new companies, NeXT (which would later be purchased by Apple, granting Jobs his executive position back in the company he founded) and Pixar (which would later sell to Disney for $7.4 billion), and met whom he calls the love of his life—his wife.[26] In his 2005 commencement address at Stanford University he said, "I didn't see it then, but it turned out that getting fired from Apple was the best thing that could have ever happened to me. . . I'm pretty sure none of this would have happened if I hadn't been fired from Apple. It was awful tasting medicine, but I guess the patient needed it."

Jobs's story shows us how there are seeds of opportunity in our difficulties and that we can indeed find benefits to the most chaotic periods of our lives. Unfortunately, though, modern views aren't cultured to interpret difficulty as chances for development. Instead, emphasis is placed on either of the two extremes: avoiding challenge altogether or outright clashing against it with brute-force—never the middle way, where one harmonically *works with* the challenge.

When we view the world as separate from us, it's not unusual to think the world is something we must command and conquer. Consequently, it's not unusual to become a dog in a dog-eat-dog world. The problem with this mindset is that it creates behaviors where we force our way through life rather than flowing with life, thus expending more energy than required and undergoing greater suffering than necessary.

Any people who have immersed themselves into a practice long enough have experienced a natural state of flow. It's a perfect state of seemly, automatic motion where skill and challenge wonderfully meet—the individual is "in the zone." Fully immersed and completely involved, there's natural energy keeping the practitioner focused with a sincere sense of enjoyment. Rather than performing the dance, the dancer becomes the performance; rather than playing the music, the musician becomes the song. In flow, the entrepreneur brings the vision to fruition by becoming the vision.

Work is only an idea living in a person's mind; it is idle without energy behind it. Work can't work itself. Though, the moment a person does engage with this thing called "work," he or she breathes life into it, and their breath carries with it all the corresponding ideas that come with their concept of "work." In other words, we inject an image of who we are into the process. If we're disordered, our *work* will be sloppy. If we're tired, our *work* will lag or skip a beat. However, if we're focused, our *work* will be accurate. And if we're completely at peace, things will gracefully complete themselves.

This awareness of natural flow states is lacking in our culture; that's why people often try to use force to strong-arm their desires into fruition; they try to control nature. However, nature isn't something people can force their way with—not in their practice, not in their work, and certainly not in their relationships. It would be like trying to force gravity. People who have tried imposing their will onto gravity have learned that what goes up must come down. People who have tried to conquer the ways of nature have tasted the bitterness of failure. The correct way to get what you want is to work *with* nature, *with* gravity, like the Wright brothers did when they invented the world's first successful airplane. This is the principal behind many of the most effective and practical East Asian martial arts, such as judo and jujitsu.

The Game of the Follower

Any time we reinforce the belief that circumstances mold our lives—that things happen *to* us—we further shape our minds into viewing the world as an enemy. We develop thoughts like, "Forces beyond my grasp govern my life," "Those who know more than I do have control over me," "I'm just born unlucky," or, "This is my fate." Hence, we cultivate attitudes that weaken our creative abilities and hurt our self-image; we grow to see ourselves as puppets—victims in a chaotic world ruled by those with more money, power, secrets, and abilities that we don't have access to.

Those who view life in this way live in survival mode (which we will discuss further in a later chapter); to them, existence means meeting basic physiological needs and enduring times of isolation "until things change." People with this attitude define reality strictly with their senses: with what they can see, hear, smell, taste, and feel. Their attention is glued to the outer world because *that's* where the threats lurk. They fear both loss and the unknown. Coming from a stress-filled place of lack and limitations, they interpret reality with a jaded lens. These individuals have allowed previous scars to become ever-present reminders of what happens when they risk anything.

This worldview of "survival" is deteriorating to people's mental faculties and their awareness of the part of themselves that knows and wants what's best—it works against their natural wiring for success. That guiding voice inside us drowns; then, without a strong internal compass, we become easily distracted and easily influenced.

Deep down, people know what's best for themselves; however, most allow their minds to deceive themselves into avoiding accountability. Carrying the shame of having experienced a setback they did not grow from, these individuals seek refuge in superficial activities. And when those are no longer enough to fill the inner void, they turn to devices and substances—anything to escape the reality they're faced with. These people become easily affected by the external world. Unable to deal with the world's harsh criticisms, they conform to society's expectations to avoid further shame. They do what those around them are doing and listen to what those around them are listening to with no consideration of their personal paths in life. Consequently, their relationships indicate bonds of codependency and ultimately turn into a game of *follow the follower*.

The fear of being alone, the fear of shame, and the fear of confronting a disharmonious sense of reality distance people's characters from their potential. We see this with those who blindly follow others into career paths or business ventures. Seeing a friend cash in on an investment, they believe there to be a shortcut to wealth, so they jump on board so as to not miss out on the opportunity—only later finding themselves trapped with a sense of meaninglessness.

Playing the game of follow the follower holds an individual back from experiencing life to the fullest. It sets the impression that there is no power within us and that we must wait for favorable circumstances, lucky situations, or other people to help us reach new heights. When we have this mindset, we lack a sense of purpose and cannot create long-term visions for our lives. As a result, we have little understanding about how to effectively structure our days to positively impact our situations. We turn hollow inside and continue to aimlessly drift in a passive manner through life with no goal in mind.

The Courage to Grow

To avoid playing follow the follower, to cultivate a healthy state of mind, we need personal empowerment, and that starts with courage. When we don't confront our insecurities in loneliness, we conform and continue passing through life feeling irrelevant and unconnected. We feel stuck when it comes to changing our life patterns, our ability to adapt to our environment declines, and our capacity to develop a richer, more satisfying personality is stunted. From this mental plateau, our times of solitude turn into times filled with anxiety and depression; we feel completely powerless and uncertain of our ability to assert ourselves and face the challenges we're presented with.

The courageous path, the path of growth, embraces solitude and explores the self—the imagination, beliefs, perceptions, thoughts, and more. The courageous path analyzes what it means to be *this* human being.

Increasing our self-awareness not only gives us insights into our natural strengths and abilities but also makes us more mindful of the present moment and our circumstances. This mindfulness allows the deep wisdom in our bodies to speak to us using the form of language we've learned to call *intuition*.

When we heed our intuition, we become more capable of identifying, interpreting, and dealing with the natural emotions of life, and we access more profound realms of gratitude, joy, and peace. Simultaneously, we also learn to recognize that feelings like guilt, regret, fear, anxiety, and despair are signals from our higher Selves that we're not adequately processing our environments' conditions and meeting our needs.

Those who have opened themselves up as sincere seekers of Truth sooner or later catch a glimpse of this higher Self. It conveys an unfulfilled potential which has a fundamental connection to the natural flow of nature. This higher Self is an inner guide; a birthright that no one is left without. It's the (warrior's) Spirit, which is available to anyone who believes in Him.

When people live life with the guidance of Self, they let go of personal gratification, but their hearts are always filled. There's no concern about the praise or approval of others, nor about personal gain, just pure intentions, and a clear vision of what turns out to be the best for all. This is what enabled Steve Jobs to bounce back from the most devastating moment in his career—he was following his intuition and doing what he loved. His happiness grew once more because of his progress in his personal plans. Overcoming his doubt time and time again, he developed a strong belief in his abilities—he didn't rely on position, authority, or anything outside himself.

With more respect for ourselves and more confidence in our innate ability to direct the course of our lives, we empower ourselves and develop the courage to view the world through a lens of abundance. In other words, as an alternative to viewing the world with a lens of lack and limitation—as if there's not enough to go around—we realize the limitless opportunities available to us all, and we take a more proactive approach to life. Heeding our intuition and taking the courageous path is the process of self-actualization.

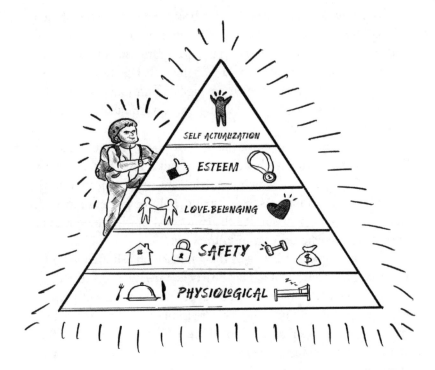

The Need for Self-Actualization

Self-actualization is a term coined by Abraham Maslow, an American psychologist who stressed the importance of focusing on positive qualities and not treating people as "bags of symptoms."[27] Maslow devoted most of his time to studying those who excelled in life rather than to studying mental illness like his peers did. His theory of psychological health was grounded in human beings' responsibility to fulfill their innate needs. His model shows us that the healthiest and most successful among us are motivated by "self-actualization"—growth toward the fulfillment of our highest needs; particularly, growth toward meaning in life. Ultimately, Maslow found that his theory was the groundwork that set the foundation for humans to create a wholesome lifestyle. His theory gives us a logical, easy-to-follow blueprint of standard needs necessary for a psychologically healthy life.

Maslow argued that there are five stages of human needs that motivate our behavior. In order, the stages are physiological needs, safety, love and belonging, esteem, and self-actualization. Our physiological needs are the needs to survive. As human animals, we instinctively secure these needs first. The moment we get these needs met, we'll become motivated to reach the next level: safety. For our safety, we look to earn, build, and create shelter to protect ourselves from danger. This includes physical safety, being of service, having enough resources, and being able to secure the resources we've already gathered. Next, during the stage where we seek love and belonging, we form desires for a sense of connection and a place to fit in. We find those with shared interests and build bonds with them. At the next stage, we look to build healthy self-esteem and to raise our self-confidence. We look toward accomplishments and meeting challenges. Our aim is to recognize and realize our strengths—to become people who are worthy of respect from both ourselves and others.

After we satisfy the first four needs—after we can breathe, eat, drink, sleep, feel safe, feel a part of a supportive group, and feel unique—then we can make the most progress in the self-actualization stage.

In the stage of self-actualization, we cultivate a desire to become the most we can be, and in doing so we allow ourselves to reach our creative potential. Thus, we access the deeper realms of creativity, spontaneity, and problem solving. We adjust our morals and ethics, and we discover penetrating truths that further increase our awareness of our Selves and the ongoings of reality. From there, not only does our desire to make more meaningful contributions to the world increase, but our ability to adapt to our environment grows, and we learn to better flow with circumstances to reach our goals. When we self-actualize, we fill the inner void and create the meaning we all long for in life.

Unless we're growing in this stage and becoming what we're capable of being, we're not likely to experience happy and fulfilling lives. Therefore, we have no choice but to confront our feelings of loneliness.

Our psychological states depend on the perspectives we have about ourselves and about the world around us. When we understand this, we realize our problems are not riches, reputation, or influence, but rather our problems are the beliefs we have and the ways we think.

Challenges and moments of solitude are there for us to embrace, and when we embrace them, we allow ourselves to locate real power within. This inner power puts us on our paths toward self-development, aligns us with our higher nature, and allows us to play leadership roles as the creators of life's circumstances—becoming the Self that leads the self, revealing the warrior's Spirit within and letting it shine through.

"You can't connect the dots looking forward, you can only connect them looking backwards. So you have to trust that the dots will somehow connect in the future. You have to trust in something—your gut, destiny, life, karma, whatever. Because believing that the dots will connect down the road will give you the confidence to follow your heart, even when it leads you off the well-worn path. And that will make all the difference. . . . And most important, have the courage to follow your heart and intuition. They somehow already know what you truly want to become." —Steve Jobs[28]

Meditation is essential for understanding ourselves.

7 EXPLORING WHAT'S INSIDE

Four monks decided to meditate silently without speaking for two weeks. They lit a candle as a symbol of their practice and began. By nightfall on the first day, the candle flickered and then went out.

The first monk said, "Oh, no! The candle is out."

The second monk said, "We're not supposed to talk!"

The third monk said, "Why must you two break the silence?"

The fourth monk laughed and said, "Ha! I'm the only one who didn't speak."[29]

Memento Mori

It's our deepest longing to be happy and to live a life truly worth living so that at any moment, we can face death with straight eyes, and our spirits will leave without shame or regret.

"Today is a good day to die."

Does it truly feel that way, though? Most people have an enormous fear of death and rarely enjoy discussing the topic. Usually, death crosses their minds only when life's circumstances force it to. As a result, people suffer just thinking about it. To them, death is an awful thing.

Nevertheless, it seems clear to me that those who remain conscious of their mortality are actually better equipped to live a fuller life. In the ancient Greek philosophy, Stoicism, the student uses the concept of death to gain strength and energy and also to create priority and meaning; the idea is a constant reminder to not waste any time in the day on things that are superficial or insignificant. A popular Latin expression used by modern Stoics today is *memento mori*, meaning "remember death." The phrase is believed to have originated from an ancient Roman tradition. After a major military victory, the triumphant generals were paraded through town in a chariot drawn by four horses to the cheers of the masses. They were worshiped, viewed as divine warriors and sometimes even as gods. This ceremony could sometimes last the entire day, and there wasn't a more desired honor to have. However, riding in the same chariot, standing right behind the idolized general, was a servant. This servant's sole responsibility would be to continually whisper into the general's ear at the peak of his victory, "*Respice post te! Hominem te esse memento! Memento mori!*" which roughly translates to, "Look behind you! Remember that you are but a man! Remember that you'll die!"

This idea of contemplating our death isn't an awful thing but a powerful tool to create urgency, meaning, and priorities in life. Ultimately, it adjusts our perspectives and adds to our happiness by treating life as a gift—because death makes life purposeful, not pointless.

Even better off are those who *prepare* for death by regularly shedding unnecessary parts of themselves, like the snake that sheds its skin. This shedding requires a practice—a discipline. It takes consistent effort, and, unfortunately, it's consistent effort that the average person isn't willing to invest—and that's why their lives remain average at best. Like brushing teeth only once and expecting a white smile, the average conditioned mind hopes for long-term changes from unpredictable short, sporadic advances. It shows in our data; people spend almost five times more on lottery tickets than on books. Instead of investing in slow but guaranteed improvements in thinking and decision-making, our culture is more likely to bet

everything on chance, hoping to be the one in almost fourteen million who wins the lottery. Rather than developing themselves and creating lasting strategies, conditioned minds are set on finding the next get-rich-quick scheme. It's a quick-fix mentality sprouting from worry—the natural behavior of an untrained mind.

By neglecting to take complete ownership of the mind we allow our intelligence to be easily highjacked. Part of this dilemma stems from our upbringing in current education systems. We're taught to view our body parts as separate, trainable muscles, but the mind isn't given the same consideration. Most of the focus is on only one aspect of the mind's capabilities—memory. Very little attention, if any, is given to training the mind's imagination, will, intuition, perception, and reason. Consequently, many of us don't reach any reasonable level of fulfillment because we're stuck at points of comfort and familiarity and don't realize how much better things can actually be. We're not thrilled with our lives, but neither are we sad. Cruising through our days in routines, on autopilot, we find just enough distractions and dopamine rushes to keep ourselves going, and without adequate curiosity or pain, we continue with a view of happiness and fulfillment dependent upon external conditions.

We sometimes become so invested in who we think we are that there is little desire to make any actual change—to take charge of the mind, becoming someone new. It's as if when we were born, we were each given a map for life; however, while we've stubbornly been trying to apply the maps in our current lands, they are actually maps of foreign countries.

This misperception happens when we cannot notice deeper aspects of ourselves and the ways in which we've been influenced—whether by parents, peers, or society. We have spent a great deal of time with things we think matter to us but actually don't. Then, we have gotten used to the way things are, closing up to any new situations that could potentially reveal genuine sources of happiness—from within.

The Courage to Change

Nobody wants to admit they've been wasting their entire lives following the wrong map. Even if the problem is brought to their attention, very few people have the courage to accept the reality, let alone do something about it. In the previous chapter, we discussed how personal empowerment begins with courage and how it's important to confront our insecurities and feelings of loneliness, to embrace solitude and explore ourselves. To expand on that, let's discuss a more practical perspective on the theme of courage.

To many, courage is something you either have or don't. However, courage can be developed, like a muscle. It's a feature of one of the mind's faculties, the will. Courage is active and lively; it's not "I came, I saw, I conquered"; it's "I showed up, I struggled, I got 0.01%

better for next time." Courage is not the absence of fear; it is doing something despite fear. Courage means wondering, "What if, what if, what if," and *still* pushing forward. Ultimately, courage means persevering even through the periods that are difficult.

Just by slightly adjusting their understanding of what courage is, people can begin building enough inner confidence to prepare themselves to endure major transformations.

Change can be a tough process; there are always periods that will seem unbearably difficult. That's why few people can voluntarily make real, lasting changes.[30] Usually, life's circumstances pressure people to change, yet even that type of change is infrequent.

This general unwillingness to change is due to the fact that there are parts of our self—the ego—that resist the unknown. Meaning that, along with the idea of inner confidence, there's almost always present on some level an inner resistance that can be devilishly clever. It has no power of its own and is fueled by our own fears. Creative enough to formulate deceptive mental traps, this inner resistance plays on our doubts to keep us from progressing. It can use methods such as rationalizing, stimulating greater fears and anxieties, prioritizing distractions, strengthening the voices of our inner critics, and anything else to keep things as they are. On top of that, if people aren't prepared for the advancements they do manage to make, this inner resistance can bring them right back to where they were—like when lottery winners waste all their winnings.

The desire to break free from this battle with the force of inner resistance follows the same pattern as the desire to improve ourselves; the part of us that wants to break free is the same part that's chained but doesn't have the key. On a conscious level we can decide to be better, but until we apply the conscious mind to repeatedly program the subconscious—the self-image, which is the origin for about ninety-five percent of our behavior—we'll keep behaving in the same ways and experiencing the same results.[31]

What's important is that we realize when we're in a battle with the force of inner resistance. More often than not, its first line of defense is to use rationalizations to close our minds. Whenever we're in a closed state of mind, we're likely to reject transformative information, rationalizing with "I disagree" or "I already knew that." We're quick to dismiss something if it doesn't match our current belief system or if we believe we understand it enough—"That's stupid" or "I know." We don't give ourselves a chance to allow for a deeper understanding; and in life there's always a deeper layer of meaning.

To counter ideas fostering a closed mind, we can redirect our attention toward our desire to make progress and then further reinforce a meaning to our situation that will encourage our development. If we're using our conscious will to focus on our improvements—no matter how small—and we're reaffirming our intentions for continuous growth, we cultivate an attitude of openness. From there, we can trust our reticular activating system to pick up on what's necessary to further promote the changes we're looking to make. All that's necessary of us is to trust in our inner guide by not rejecting or judging any piece of information.

"Everything you need is already inside you"—by accepting this perspective, we see that the mystery of life is not a problem to be solved but a reality to be experienced.

This viewpoint may be challenging to grasp at first because of our remarkable ability to think about our own thoughts. The term is labeled *metacognition*—the mental faculty to become aware of our own awareness, to examine our own processes of thoughts and feelings. Metacognition is the ability to observe self and environment. It gives us the capability to create a mental separation between thoughts and thinker and allows us to identify as something different, something greater.

The Necessity of Meditation

Metacognition is trained through meditation, the art of quietly being with yourself, distraction-free. Meditation is essential for understanding ourselves. Imagine being in a completely dark room with a flashlight, and you can only see the small area you're pointing the light at. Now imagine that dark room is your mind, and what you've revealed with the flashlight is your awareness. Meditation is a practice that gradually increases the brightness and scope of that flashlight to reveal more and more.

From a practical approach, meditation is the mental exercise of allowing our thoughts to float away like balloons, only to identify with the blank spaces in between. It's a training of the self to stop automatically identifying with thoughts. For instance, if the mind were a highway and thoughts were vehicles, meditation would be the practice of simply observing the cars go by and, rather than chasing after them—which would be a never-ending pursuit—to connect with the emptiness in the road instead.

With so much going on in our lives, we might worry that we can't quiet our minds, and that's true. The desire to quiet one's mind will only increase the chatter and bring about more friction. However, it's less about quieting the mind and more about being aware of our mind. The easiest way into the meditative state is by simply closing our eyes and wholeheartedly listening. While staying observant of the breath, we should open ourselves up to the general sounds around us, as if the sounds of cars passing, wind blowing, and birds chirping are background music at a café.

The effort is to not judge or name the sounds ("That sound was a car!"), because this is likely to start a chain of thoughts. ("Sounded like a sports car; maybe it was a Mustang or a Corvette; it's probably letting off harmful fumes; there's so much pollution in our environment . . . ") Instead, we should allow these sounds and thoughts to ring in our ears and then go. The ears should hear whatever they want to hear without the thoughts interfering.

This may be a challenging endeavor for some. When we close our eyes, we dive into the inner world and are faced with who we are. If we're experiencing a heightened sense of discomfort, it's likely that there's conflict in our lives that we've avoided attending to; there's trouble with who we feel we are—there're decisions we're making that aren't aligned with who we believe ourselves to be, outcomes in our past that we haven't adequately processed, or circumstances (fears) that we're not confronting. Especially in these scenarios, the voices inside will go on automatically, and those with the wrong idea of meditation will sense frustration within themselves and think they're not making any progress; they'll think meditation *isn't working* for them because they *can't relax*. However, particularly in these moments, it's important to remember that thoughts are not meant to be repressed by force; that will produce the same results as trying to get a baby to stop crying by yelling at it. Instead, again, we should simply look at these thoughts as part of the background noise. If the mind insists on thinking, let it think, and just watch it do its thing while calmly returning focus to the breath—trying to synchronize the duration of the inhale with the exhale, all while really *feeling* the aspects of the breath: its texture, temperature, how it expands and contracts the belly and rib cage, and so on. After a while, the sounds around us and the thoughts and emotions inside us eventually come together. This bringing together of the inner and outer worlds is sincere progress.

Several studies have linked meditation practices to significant differences in the thickness or density of gray matter in the brain. The outcomes of these studies show that the practice of meditation results in changed levels of activity in brain regions associated with focus, anxiety, anger, depression, and fear, and in the regenerative abilities of the body.[32] Its benefits include, but are not limited to: a quietness of mind, a sensation of tranquility and equanimity, and increased levels of energy and creativity. With meditative practices, we can literally heal and strengthen the parts of our brains that aid in building full and happy lives.

Moreover, these studies show that we can actively rework areas within ourselves that hold us back—we can go beyond ourselves to view our circumstances objectively, with greater clarity. It makes sense: the less sensory information comes into the brain, the less computing it must do. Cutting off the senses from the outside world means we're only left with the internal world of thoughts, feelings, and emotions. And the more we can tune out the world outside us, the more we can work out the mental muscle—our concentration—that turns our attention to the world inside us; as a result, we eventually make the inner world the more powerful one, and we become less affected by forces outside us. In this sense, meditation is a workout for the mind like lifting weights is a workout for the body. As we practice different techniques of meditation, we actively train the various faculties (or muscles) of the mind (willpower, imagination, intuition, reasoning, perception, and memory). This is something most people do not realize about meditation: that it's practical and has a significant impact on our day-to-day lives.

Meditation has become common in the West, but it seems many have yet to develop the right perspective about it. People are using it as a practice to quiet their minds, to relax, and to become better individuals. But we also hear of businesspeople meditating to bring about better innovations and to make more money; of doctors meditating because it will help them operate better; of lawyers meditating to build better cases; of athletes meditating for higher performance and victory. Many people use unique methods of meditation to reach the specific results they desire. While meditation is certainly a powerful means for centering one's self for productivity and achievement, it can be so much more if approached correctly.

Failing to appreciate that *having* comes naturally as a result of *doing*, many people are attracted to the mindset of meditating to *have* rather than meditating to *do*. Ultimately, these motives for practicing meditation stimulate the belief that "the purpose of meditation is to have no thoughts." Coming from this standpoint, where a goal is in mind, we prohibit true meditation because our minds are directed out of the present moment and into the future—into the goal—in an "I'll be happy when . . . " manner.

We already know intellectually that the future is a concept; it doesn't exist. But it's only when we maintain our meditative practice long enough, with the right view, that we can feel the real magnitude of this realization: *tomorrow never comes.*

The true benefits of meditation only reveal themselves when our practice is for the sake of practice. Instead of viewing meditation as a *thing*, we should view it as a movement—a movement into the entire question of our being and of the lives we lead. It's an inquiry into our deepest thoughts, beliefs, desires, behaviors, and so on. Meditation questions the self-images we've built, our images of others, and our images of the roles we occupy in life.

These images carry weight and are often the causes of our stagnation and the reasons we don't grow. As the brilliant French novelist Marcel Proust expressed, "The real voyage of discovery consists not in seeking new landscapes, but in having new eyes." We can develop these new eyes and become aware of the images—of ourselves—through the powers of meditation, which is critical for a full and happy life.

The Beginner's Mind

Like we talked about in chapter six, the most devastating moment in Steve Jobs's career, when he was fired from his own company at Apple, was just what he needed. Jobs's success had created a negative impact on who he thought he was. His fame and achievements, as noteworthy as they were, clouded his mind and caused him much unrest. He explained in a speech, "The heaviness of being successful was replaced by the lightness of being a beginner again, less sure about everything. It freed me to enter one of the most creative periods of my life."[33]

In the practice of Zen, *shoshin* is a term for developing an open mind, a "beginner's mind," for approaching life with eagerness and a lack of preconceptions. Shunryū Suzuki, a Zen master, expressed the importance of the beginner's mind with this observation: "In the beginner's mind there are many possibilities, but in the expert's there are few."[34] As we become better at certain things and our knowledge about given subjects grows, our minds naturally close up. It's the trap most experts fall into if they haven't developed their beginner's mind. They reject new or different information; what they really want is to reconfirm the information they already have. This eventually creates turmoil within the individual, especially when the information they have begins to fail them.

This is what happened to the leaders of the businesses of Block-buster, Boarders, Toys R Us, Circuit City, Kodak and countless others. They couldn't see the changes our society was going through, and as a result, they couldn't keep up with the times at hand. Accordingly, they failed to innovate and adapt in time to future-proof their businesses. It was a natural consequence of the expert's mind.

We must always be open to the idea that our ways of doing things might not be the only ways and that there might be considerably better ways. Having the beginner's mind means we're willing to consider and learn any piece of information as something new and to entertain any idea, regardless of whether we've been exposed to it before, as if we were a child exposed to something for the first time. Unless we admit that we're capable of having blind spots, we'll never notice the clues that point toward them. Stephen Hawking voiced this same concern: "The greatest enemy of knowledge is not ignorance; it is the illusion of knowledge."

It's only when we're making these honest reflections on our self that we truly shed layers of illusions and find the meaning to our meditations. It's at this point that we can truly confront our feelings of loneliness and turn periods of anxiety-filled solitude into periods of rejuvenation and revitalization. Simply put, unless we've established some sense of understanding for the many confusions, contradictions, and struggles in our lives, we have not really begun sincere meditation.

It should become increasingly apparent that, even though we're wired for success, we are all cognitively flawed. Yet, this realization will feel like a form of enlightenment, like knowing that although we seem to all be flawed in some way, at least we have the blessing to know that much. From there we can appreciate the idea that our basic and fundamental purpose in life is happiness—happiness from the growth we experience when we navigate life's trails.

With our understanding of ourselves and our happiness, whether or not we approach death with straight eyes is completely up to us. Our duty is simply to discover and cultivate the things that lead to our development and discard the things that don't, and we can accomplish these tasks through daily meditations and reflections. These practices will gradually increase our awareness and understanding of the ways in which we're operating—it will help us train our metacognitive abilities.

With improved metacognition, our thinking about our thinking will help us make greater sense of our life experiences, and our rationalizations will be less of a hindrance to our objectives. Furthermore, we'll better know what truly matters to us and what we really want.

We each make a handful of key decisions that affect the courses of our lives. It often goes unstated, but the choice to be happy and to live our lives with purpose is just as significant as any other choice.

Tao means how: how things happen, how things work. Tao is the single principle underlying all creation. Tao is God. Tao cannot be defined, because it applies to everything. You cannot define something in terms of itself. If you can define a principle, it is not Tao.

Tao is a principle. Creation, on the other hand, is a process. That is all there is: principle and process, how and what. All creation unfolds according to Tao. There is no other way.

Tao cannot be defined, but Tao can be known. The method is meditation, or being aware of what is happening. By being aware of what is happening, I begin to sense how it is happening. I begin to sense Tao. To become aware of what is happening, I must pay attention with an open mind. I must set aside my personal prejudices or bias. Prejudice people see only what fits those prejudices.

The method of meditation works, because principle and process are inseparable. All process reveals the underlying principle. This means that I can know Tao. I can know God. By knowing Tao, I know how things happen.[35]

—Tao Te Ching, *Lao Tzu, verse 1*

If you're happy, you can genuinely enjoy pleasures; if you're not happy, pleasures can take over your life.

8 CHOOSING INNER CONTENTMENT

A big, tough samurai once went to see a little monk.

"Monk!" he barked, in a voice accustomed to instant obedience. "Teach me about heaven and hell!"

The monk looked up at the mighty warrior and replied with utter disdain, "Teach you about heaven and hell? I couldn't teach you about anything. You're dumb. You're dirty. You're a disgrace, an embarrassment to the samurai class. Get out of my sight. I can't stand you."

The samurai got furious. He shook, red in the face, speechless with rage. He pulled out his sword and prepared to slay the monk.

Looking straight into the samurai's eyes, the monk said softly, "That's hell."

The samurai froze, realizing the compassion of the monk who had risked his life to show him hell! He put down his sword and fell to his knees, filled with gratitude.

The monk said softly, "And that's heaven."[36]

The Desire to Be Happy

Do you know what you want from life? It's probably the same thing I want. Deep down inside, each of us wants the same thing, even though very few of us seem to know what it is.

Sure, if we ask around, we'll probably hear that people want more money, fame, or other luxuries and pleasures. However, when we really use our imagination and contemplate our answers, we'll probably admit that the first few responses we come up with are answers to things we only think we want, things we've probably been conditioned to want.

This doesn't take away from the legitimacy of these desires. However, beneath the surface are deeper needs. For example, if we want money, what we could really be longing for is empowerment or freedom; often money is what we think we want when our lives are missing a feeling of security. Other times, we want the feeling of having the ability to choose or the feeling of having the ability to help others. These are common underlying feelings.

We all want love and connection—good quality of life and good relationships.

We want comfort and variety—nice toys to play with and fine dining to enjoy.

We want a sense of significance—to feel like we belong to and are needed in the world.

We want to grow and have ways in which we can contribute, and we want to feel confident in our ability to creatively express ourselves. We want to know that we have the power to make positive changes in the world around us. We want to look forward to tomorrow. Typically, we want the *feeling* we can get from the things we want, not the things themselves. We've labeled this feeling *happiness*.

Those desires are generally what comes to mind when we think of happiness; but then again, what does that all mean? What is happiness?

To some, the answer closely relates to feelings of pleasure; but it's essential to differentiate happiness from pleasure. Happiness is a natural part of us all. It's stable and persistent; it can stay regardless of life's ups and downs. It enables us to be more effective, have better ideas, and cultivate better relationships. Pleasure, on the other hand, is short lived and often accompanied by pain. If you're happy, you can genuinely enjoy pleasures; if you're not happy, pleasures can take over your life. As the ancient Greek philosopher Epicurus said, "Pleasure is the beginning and end of the blessed life."

So what does happiness mean to us?

In the Western part of the world, happiness seems to be imprecise, vague, and ungraspable. The English word itself—"happy"—is derived from the Old Norse word *hap*, meaning "chance" or "luck."[37] It's no mystery why people would commonly see happiness as something created through external circumstances.

We can train our minds to expand our perspectives on happiness. When I talk about training the mind, I'm not only referencing Western academic terms (be it *cognitive ability* or *intellectual capacity*) but also the gut, mind, and heart, and patience and equanimity. This training would include a better understanding of our feelings but also an inner discipline toward the goal of transforming our attitudes and reactions. Ultimately this training is meant to help us develop completely new outlooks on life, ones that include happiness, growth, and a genuine sense of independent fulfillment.

Training the mind to develop a greater sense of happiness is a real objective, and there are solid steps to achieve and maintain it. It starts the same way that any other effort toward an objective would start—by first studying it, then by doing the things that allow us to reach it, then by doing less of what takes us away from it.

The Dangers of Comparing

We must accept the idea that each person's happiness is determined by a state of mind, not by external conditions. How we interpret a situation, what type of meaning we assign to it, and how we feel about that interpretation are more important than the situation itself. We derive happiness from how content we feel about our current lives. Our moment-to-moment happiness is determined by

our attitude toward our life. Happiness is cultivated from within and is available at any time.

Being that our outlooks on existence are so important, inner discipline, especially in terms of our perception, reasoning, and imagination, plays an increasingly important role.

One characteristic of an untrained mind is its unfruitful use of the imagination to compare and compete. Whether we're comparing ourselves to our past selves or to other people, our cognitive ability to compare has a direct influence on our levels of satisfaction. The act of using our imagination to compare has an immediate impact on our emotions. For example, when we compare ourselves to others who seem smarter or better looking, or who have more perceived success, we can create a breeding ground for jealousy, envy, or frustration within ourselves, leading to feelings of discontentment and unhappiness. However, when we compare with those who have less, the opposite can happen; it may make us immediately more grateful, consequently increasing our levels of satisfaction on our own lives' situations.

It's important to note that although comparing ourselves to others who seem to be in worse circumstances can increase our levels of satisfaction on our own situations, cultivating our emotions in this way can lead to pride, condescension, and a general unwillingness to help others. Drawing comparisons is always risky. The idea I'm trying to get across is that the active mind understands by comparing. When we think about how good we have it, we're happier; when we become attached to our desires, we're less satisfied and experience a sense of inner turmoil or suffering.

It's like when our wages jump from twenty dollars an hour to forty dollars an hour: initially, we feel happy; we're comparing our newly increased income to the lower wages we were earning once before. But because the feeling was triggered from an external source, that feeling will inevitably wear off. We'll adapt and get used to the new wage. Then the day will come when we notice opportunities for sixty dollars an hour, and at that moment forty dollars an hour just won't feel sufficient anymore.

The Need for Inner Contentment

Jesus, one of the greatest teachers to walk the face of our planet, taught, "Man shall not live by bread alone."[38] Wealth alone cannot guarantee happiness. We've seen on many occasions that even some of the most financially developed individuals experience unrest, escapism, sadness, depression, frustration, anger, and even hatred.

What good are possessions if we're not at peace within ourselves? The depressed individual has little interest in activities. Those who wish to escape from their realities do not fully engage with their environment. Those angry and filled with hatred can throw and break things in frustration. Even our own friends and family seem cold, distant, and outright annoying when we're irritated and unhappy. What use would belongings be to a person in this condition?

Although a healthy financial life is important, happiness starts with a state of mind. With effort and self-discipline, external situations become less important. This is true even in the modern world, where desires and the general noise of society can flood our awareness.

The critical ingredient to being happy even in a materialistic society is inner contentment, and there are two methods to achieve it. One, we can obtain everything we want and view our lives as perfect; or two, we can appreciate everything we already have and focus on the things we can do. Since obtaining everything and keeping it in a perfect state is not within our control, we should be focusing on the second method.

We cultivate inner contentment—which should not be confused with complacency—through our daily choices. We don't always choose what's best for us, because the "right choice" is often perceived as the toughest choice to make. Having to say "no" to something easy but wrong can, in the moment, make us feel like we are missing out, especially if others are saying "yes." However, we must structure our decisions within the scope of "Will this decision truly bring me peace of mind and happiness?" or "Will my future self thank me for making this decision?" When the answer to each of those questions is *no*, by deciding to say "no" to the easy wrong, we can recognize that we're moving *toward* something good, not away—effectively countering the feeling of missing out.

A truly successful outcome is one where we're at peace with ourselves and with our decisions, without our sense of security coming from any outside source. Without a foundation of contentment, it's easy to fall into the idea that self-worth is based on material possessions, influence, position, and success—betting our sense of inner contentment on a fortune that may or may not be there in the next moment.

By acknowledging that we have the power to choose to be happy or not, our sense of self-worth and dignity increases; and when we change our outlooks about ourselves, we see others in a different light, becoming warmer and more compassionate toward them. In the long run, self-contentment helps us to make more meaningful connections with others. We lift others as we lift ourselves.

By training our minds to be content with our lives and decisions, we cultivate lifestyles that lead to sincere happiness and fulfillment. The more content we are with our decisions and our lives, the more our self-worth and confidence increase, and the less we compare ourselves to others. When we are content, we appreciate being distinct human beings living in a world with other distinct human beings. Our gratitude for our differences increases. We love ourselves for who we are, and we open our hearts and spread healing. We become happy.

Fame or integrity: which is more important? Money or happiness: which is more valuable? Success or failure: which is more destructive?

If you look to others for fulfillment, you will never truly be fulfilled. If your happiness depends on money, you will never be happy with yourself.

Be content with what you have; rejoice in the way things are. When you realize there is nothing lacking, the whole world belongs to you.

—Tao Te Ching, *Lao Tzu, verse 44*

"It is possible to change our experience of life, no matter our age, condition, or circumstances.

9 MOLDING THE BRAIN

Two monks were washing their bowls in the river when they noticed a scorpion that was drowning. One monk immediately scooped it up and set it upon the bank. In the process he was stung. He went back to washing his bowl and again the scorpion fell in. The monk saved the scorpion and was again stung. The other monk asked him, "Friend, why do you continue to save the scorpion when you know its nature is to sting?"

"Because," the monk replied, "to save it is my nature."[39]

The Nature of Humans

We all want to be happy and healthy, and our human minds and bodies operate better when we feel positive emotions like peace and gratitude. A calm and joyful state of mind is incredibly valuable to our wellbeing, just as anger and fear can be incredibly destructive.

Our current positions in life are in accordance with our habitual chains of thought. As humans, each of us is able to change our state of mind. We do so by using our willpower to direct our focus to embrace neutral or elevated emotional states. There will be more on this in the next chapter, but for now it's important to note that the brain doesn't know the difference between an emotion created by an experience we have in the outside environment and an experience we are creating internally through our imagination. By using disciplined practices of concentration—done through different meditations—we have the capacity to tap into gratitude and compassion at any given moment.

Because of this innate ability, willpower allows us to control our own fates. However, this is no effortless task, especially if a person's habitual train of thought is conditioned and regularly antagonistic. There needs to be a conscious decision made to train the faculties of the mind—to harness our wiring for success and leverage it to the ends we desire.

The most powerful contributing forces to our regular thoughts are our views of ourselves and other living beings. Buddhist philosophy teaches that the essence of all sentient beings is gentle and nonaggressive. However, because of the conflicts people experience in their lives and the suffering they witness around them, many have developed the belief that human nature is more aggressive than otherwise; thankfully, this is incorrect. The world's leading scientists have confirmed that humans are naturally kind and compassionate beings.[40]

Human selflessness is no new event; early humans needed to be selfless in order to survive. We were more vulnerable to animals bigger, faster, or stronger than us until we reached the top of the food chain only about 300,000 years ago, when we first began to use fire. If not for the development of our cognitive abilities and the resulting invention of instruments and strategies, we wouldn't have survived this long. However, although intelligence is critical, human intellect developed *after* human selflessness. Because of the constant dangers, it was vital for our prehistoric ancestors to form close bonds with one another to survive. During those periods, acting for the well-being of all was a means to increase the chances of survival. These characteristics still exist within us today.

This understanding of human kindness is not common in the modern way of thinking; the idea that humans are naturally selfish, aggressive beings is fixed in cultures and philosophies. However, in the past two to three decades, many studies have shown that aggression isn't innate and that violent behaviors are actually influenced by a variety of social, biological, situational, and environmental factors.[41]

In 1986, in the Seville Statement on Violence, twenty scientists from around the world acknowledged that although violence occurs, saying that we have an inherited tendency to make war or act violently is scientifically incorrect.

Their statement contained five core ideas:

1. "It is scientifically incorrect to say that we have inherited a tendency to make war from our animal ancestors."
2. "It is scientifically incorrect to say that war or any other violent behavior is genetically programmed into our human nature."
3. "It is scientifically incorrect to say that in the course of human evolution there has been a selection for aggressive behavior more than for other kinds of behavior."
4. "It is scientifically incorrect to say that humans have a 'violent brain.'"
5. "It is scientifically incorrect to say that war is caused by 'instinct' or any single motivation."

Violence, then, is essentially a trained characteristic, and humans are not innately selfish and narcissistic—we're geared toward selfless and compassionate behaviors. When we look at the countless natural disasters that we've experienced as a species, we see strong patterns of self-sacrifice and selflessness. Consider the attacks on the World Trade Center on September 11, or the enormous floods caused by Hurricane Katrina: countless individuals risked their own lives to save people they had never met before. This type of behavior has been ingrained into us from our distant past.

The Seville Statement on Violence concludes: "Just as 'wars begin in the minds of men,' peace also begins in our minds. The same species who invented war is capable of inventing peace. The responsibility lies within each of us."[42]

The Return to Human Nature

By digging into the psychological aspects of these studies and looking at the world around us, we'll notice that egotistic individuals are more vulnerable to stress, depression, and illness—all factors contributing to a less happy lifestyle.[43] Consequently, altruism and kindness are crucial for happy living. But in order to live selflessly, we need to take responsibility for our actions and regulate our habits and thoughts.

We train our minds by willfully directing attention to more effective thoughts and emotional states. This regular practice limits negative behaviors and their consequences. A quick and easy way to do this is to change our basic assumptions about the underlying nature of human beings: we need to recognize that humans are not fundamentally threatening and aggressive but compassionate and understanding. When we alter our perspectives in this way, we open alternative possibilities for ways of life. Our relationships toward ourselves and toward the world shift dramatically; we begin to relax and trust more, ultimately creating a life where we live more at ease. As Einstein stated, "The most important decision we make is whether we believe we live in a friendly or hostile universe."

Those playing the entrepreneurial role who see the world as a hostile place will find it difficult to be driven by a cause greater than themselves. Because of the general distrust undermining their views, they'll see no reason to provide value to others other than their own gains. It's likely that they'll sacrifice quality to cut costs, try to take advantage of others, and use cunning sales and marketing tactics to mislead their customers.

Entrepreneurs are deeply connected to the infrastructure of society. As they find practical means to realize the visions they hold in their minds, they contribute stability, growth, opportunities, and so on. If they're effective in their roles, they develop and enrich the world around them, and as a result, make a profit in return. When the entrepreneur has a negative outlook towards their environment, they're likely to sooner or later experience an interesting shift in consciousness where the small component effect—profit—begins to emerge as the dominant principle. Instead of working towards the manifestation of their vision, the entrepreneur begins working to make a profit; the side effect becomes the goal. This becomes so ingrained in the individual's psyche that they begin to justify their actions in terms of profits, even at the expense sometimes of the enrichment of the infrastructure of the society or the realization of their vision. Then, they have to build an entire philosophical justification in their mind to handle the fact that their goal has shifted from something which has a social significance to something that has a personal significance. The perspective they develop makes it increasingly difficult to make a sincere commitment to their craft, let alone to actually bring their vision to fruition.

No matter how much deception, violence, or mischief we've experienced in our lives, our fundamental nature remains gentle and compassionate. We can always return to that nature by making a conscious effort to redirect the brain's reticular activating system and deep subconscious programming.

Not so long ago, scientists believed that such a return wasn't possible, that the brain couldn't change much after childhood. They supposed that the brain became hardwired and fixed by the time it reached adulthood. However, due to recent developments, we've learned that the brain can and does indeed change throughout our lives. Our brains can mold and reshape themselves. We have the phenomenal ability to reorganize neural connections between brain cells, physically changing the gray matter in our brains. In doing so, we can significantly impact our development, learning, memory, and even recovery. This fascinating process has been labeled *neuroplasticity*. We can think of the brain as an electric power grid. In this power grid, billions of pathways activate and shoot electricity through the grid as soon as we think, feel, or act in any way. The more we act in specific ways, the more the pathways associated with those actions are activated; as a result, the pathways become stronger and easier to activate. We've given this process the term *habit*.

Our brains create habits for efficiency's sake. By shaping itself in such a way as to make certain pathways stronger and others weaker, the brain creates shortcuts for itself so that electricity can reach its destination faster and in an easier fashion. Our brain is continuously looking for ways to make these electric connections faster in order to increase performance and make overall health easier to maintain. It's an incredibly powerful survival mechanism that we can leverage to our advantage.

We can cause the brain to form and strengthen new connections and weaken older ones by applying the will to think, feel, or act in new ways. For instance, we can introduce ourselves to new things and new ways. Some simple and practical examples that we can implement almost immediately include brushing our teeth with the opposite hand, putting our opposite shoe on first, or using our computer mouse with the opposite hand. Combine any of these new actions with new thoughts of compassion toward ourselves and others—because neurons that fire together wire together—and we begin to physically rewire the brain for healthier, more selfless mental states. In this way, even though most neuroplasticity is incremental and not dramatic, it can take place literally every single day of our lives.[44]

Thanks to huge advancements like functional brain imaging, we have a clearer understanding of how our brains work. We now know that it's completely possible at any age to consciously develop new habits and alter our lifestyles. Anytime we learn something new, think differently than how we're used to, practice a new task, or use our willpower to choose a different thought to think or emotion to feel, we begin to stimulate new pathways in our brains. And as we continue to stimulate these pathways, our brain's efficiency will inevitably kick in. Like pacing back and forth in the sand, we will carve out new roads to reliably travel on. At the same time, the old pathways will be used less and will weaken, allowing the new way of thinking, feeling, or doing to become the standard. Through this process, we have the power to rewire our brains.

It is possible to change our experience of life, no matter our age, condition, or circumstances. We can empower ourselves to live happier, healthier, fulfilling, self-actualized lives.

Just by forming fresh perspectives on the world we live in, we're able to make the important distinction Einstein wanted us all to make: we're able to shift our view of the universe as a hostile one to a friendly and harmonious one.

Will you?

"All human beings have an extraordinary destiny! Sometimes things bring us joy and, at other times, sadness. But these ups and downs are part of everyone's destiny. The most important thing in this existence of ours is to do something that can be of benefit to others. What we need more than anything is to develop an attitude of altruism—that is really what gives meaning to life." —Dalai Lama[45]

The things that
trigger us into
negative thoughts
and emotions can
be our greatest
teachers.

10 PROGRAMMED HUMANS

A man riding a horse suddenly came galloping quickly down the road. It seemed as though the man had somewhere important to go.

Another man, who was standing alongside the road, shouted, "Where are you going?" and the man on the horse replied,

"I don't know! Ask the horse!"[46]

The Power of Repetition

Our thoughts lead to our beliefs, and our beliefs lead to our intentions. Our intentions lead to our actions, and our actions lead to our habits. Our habits lead to our character, and our character determines our destiny.

Have you noticed which shoe you put on first? How about which leg you put through your pants first? It's usually the same one every single time. Repetition is a powerful force; it's the father of all physical, mental, and spiritual learning. As creatures of habit, we each do certain things repeatedly and then get used to doing them in those specific ways. We're each accustomed to a set of automatic behaviors, thoughts, and emotions that are reinforced through repetition—a learned set of behaviors that are nearly completely involuntary.

Each of us has a robot-like mind that functions on two different levels: the conscious and the subconscious. The conscious part of the mind is rational, analytical, and objective. Some of its faculties include reason, focus, perception, and imagination. On the other hand, the subconscious is the mind's powerhouse: it houses the self-image, the ego. It's irrational and subjective. It doesn't think on its own, and we have no conscious control over what enters it. It acts as an enormous memory bank, storing and retrieving data from literally everything that the mind has ever been exposed to. A person's subconscious makes behavior consistent by familiarizing itself with what the person thinks and feels; this gives birth to our habits.[47]

In chapter nine we talked about how repeatedly pacing back and forth in the dirt will wear out a path, creating a trail. We discussed how habits work the same way in our brains. Every time we perform a series of activities, neural circuits in our brains are activated and altered; pulses are sent through specific pathways that are directly associated with the series of activities we just performed. This is how our habits and comfort zones form. Like built-in survival mechanisms, they function to make our lives easier. They have their purposes, and their purposes are for us, not against us—unless we've made them so.

Most often people think of habits in terms of just behaviors, but there's more to it than that. Our thinking also has strong and clear patterns. For example, many people focus more of their attention on their problems, worries, and frustrations than things going well in their life. These negative thoughts lead to feelings of anxiety and guilt and to a general dissatisfaction with life.[48]

Each of our thoughts is linked to specific information circuits in the brain. When we're thinking of our problems and frustrations, our brains are activating memory circuits that are linked to specific times, people, and places. Our brains can't tell the difference between a thought and an actual event.[49] The moment we recall those thoughts and memories, we generate the feelings associated with those circuits. Thinking about potential future circumstances can feed our anxieties or our excitement. Thinking about the past can bring guilt, longing, or gratitude. This is how we create a general emotional nature—a character.

Repetitive actions such as waking up, checking messages, and carrying out routine behaviors—taking the same routes to work, seeing the same people, having the same types of discussions, accepting the same types of influences—all fire the same neural pathways and activate the same emotional triggers. This is precisely how we continue to reinforce the same self-images and remain in the same life positions.

The Science of Habits

Charles Duhigg's *The Power of Habit,* a remarkable book that explores the science behind habit creation and reformation, breaks the process of a habit down into 3 + 1 parts: cues, routines, and rewards + cravings. Cues tell the brain which habit to initiate. Cues could be a particular location, time, emotional state, person, or action or routine. If there's no exposure to a cue, there's no habit. After the cue comes a mental, emotional, or physical routine. For example, waking up in the morning cues many routines—go to the bathroom, wash up, brush your teeth, get dressed, make a cup of coffee, etc. For a smoker, completing a meal may be the cue for a smoke break. Some people experience sadness as a cue that leads to overeating or boredom as a cue that leads to the desire to shop. These combinations of cues and subsequent actions create routines. When we engage in the routines, the rewards come. Rewards help the brain determine whether the series of thoughts, feelings, and actions are worth remembering for the future. If they are, and if the rewards are particularly pleasant, cravings develop.

Scientists have discovered that in the early stages of building a habit, when the reward stage of the habit process is reached the brain receives a surge of dopamine. However, as time goes on and the habit loop is reinforced through repetition, the surge of dopamine comes before the routine is even complete. Like Pavlov's dog salivating at the sound of the bell, the reward comes as soon as a cue appears. If a person is exposed to a cue for a long-time habit, the brain shows a spike of activity before the person even begins the habitual action; and it's at that moment that we feel the craving to follow through with the particular habit loop.

This is what keeps the cycle going so that when the time comes that we consciously want to change the everyday routines that have become our lifestyles, we often don't seem to have the energy to start or follow through. The subconscious, which directs about ninety-five percent of our behavior,[50] is already programmed and comfortable with what it's used to; the self-image has adapted, and the ego wants to stay consistent with the persona it's developed. So people who cannot accept their current circumstances go on, day by day, draining themselves with internal conflict, creating the same experiences, becoming more and more mentally rigid, and stripping themselves of their own free will.

No forces outside ourselves keep us from the lives we want. We allow our brains—an organ that we know little about—to become stiff and automated in ways that work against our favor, against the life we want to create for ourselves and against the visions we have for the world.

Just like how we can't blame weights for being too heavy when we can't lift them, we can't blame anything in the external world for the ways we deal with life situations. Thankfully, like with weight training, we can get better at dealing with unfavorable conditions and unpleasant circumstances. This improvement involves plunging into change and confronting and handling the emotions and discomfort that arise when we have to deal with new or frightening experiences.

We each have the responsibility to go through these experiences of change and to practice and develop self-discipline independently of others. Unfortunately, many people despise responsibility and discipline. Many people feel they can't deal with what they need to in order to reach the positions and circumstances they want. These people feel powerless and are intimidated to create effective changes in their lives. Rollo May, author of *Man's Search for Himself*, said that it

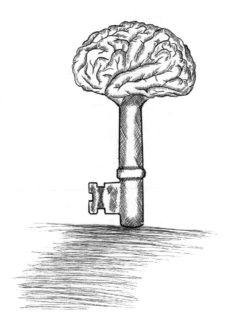

takes courage to break out of the mold of our past conditioning, but most find it easier to conform. Therefore, the opposite of courage in our society is not cowardice, it's conformity.[51]

The Key to Change

Having knowledge about how our mental mechanisms operate helps us understand the reasons why we do the things we do; and when we understand that the subconscious part of the mind contributes and directs our paths in life, we can start working to influence it in beneficial ways. That understanding empowers us in times when we decide to redirect our lives to more fruitful directions. And it's this ability to redirect our lives that gives us human beings true inner power.

So how do we change our habits?

First, we must believe that it's possible to change—even the most deeply rooted patterns. If we don't believe that change (in any aspect) is possible for us, we will direct our mind to automatically look for reasons why that change is impossible. For example, if I told you that you could accomplish your ten-year goals in a matter of one year and you didn't believe me, you'd find excuses to not even try. Your job is in the way; you're out of weight and energy levels are low; you don't know enough; you don't have the credentials to make it happen; you don't know the right people; you don't have enough resources. It will never end, and you will never take the first step. However, if you believed in the possibility, you'd direct your mind to look for ways to confirm that and it will come up with creative solutions to try to make it happen. You might hire a coach, join a program, develop new routines, find new social circles, learn new things. The possibilities are endless for the person who truly believes, because they will always direct their attention towards building the new instead of fighting the old. For this individual, mental energy is invested into saying *yes* to the new life, rather than *no* to the old life; their imagination, will, and reason is leveraged not to fight the old self, but to create and jump into a new self—one that's more aligned with what they really want from life.

Functional MRI brain scans have confirmed that our brains don't know the distinction between imagination and reality.[52] For instance, imagining playing the piano and actually playing the piano physically activate the same parts of the brain. Thanks to several studies and experiments that have proved that the brain can be fooled by the method of conscious visualization, we know how to harness the powerful forces of our conscious mind and leverage our subconscious to attain our desired circumstances.[53]

Consciously, we have the power to think any thought, but mostly we think thoughts that are in alignment with our subconscious. However, by using the conscious parts of our minds—the thinking parts—we can decide to consistently fill our minds with the thoughts and beliefs necessary for the adjustments we want to make. For example, after we've identified a cue for an undesirable habit, we can imagine ourselves experiencing the cue and instead of following through with the regular routine, to replace it with a desired routine. For instance, we can visualize ourselves getting up from the dinner table after a meal and instead of lighting up a cigarette, going for a walk or drinking some warm tea—and most importantly, feeling good about it. If we support these thoughts with positive and satisfying feelings, our brains will accept these imprints on the deeper levels, allowing us to reach the subconscious and create new, better habits.

Visualization, in this way, is incredibly powerful because, from the standpoint of the brain, we're creating new memories. When we couple images and emotions in our visualizations of our desired outcomes, we tell our brain *this is what our life is like*. From there, when we continuously show up for ourselves and practice, we program our reticular activating system to look for opportunities to confirm *this new life*. That way, when the RAS discovers a chance to make our desired outcome a reality, our brain is primed and ready to trigger us to jump into action and perform the necessary tasks to make the visualized patterns a reality.

Visualization was brought into the mainstream by the popular book and documentary called *The Secret*, which discuss what they label *The Law of Attraction*—the compelling observation that we attract into our lives that which we place our attention on most. However, many people misinterpret the message; some even believe this observation to be a law that ends all problems and cures all ailments. They believe that having kept in their mind's eye the solution or circumstances they desire, everything will fall into place for them without any action on their part. The truth of the matter is, we don't attract the things we *want*, because if we're in a state of great wanting, we're simultaneously in a state of great lacking. This situation is like nailing a chair to the ceiling and expecting gravity to lift us up into it; it's leveraging the principles backwards.

Really, *The Secret* is saying that we attract what we *are*; that's why they repeatedly express the phrase "like attracts like." Therefore, we cannot remain in the emotional state of *wanting*; we must shift our emotion into *already having*, *being*, and *experiencing*. This is the faith that puts one into an uplifted state, makes them feel deserving, aligns the RAS to spot what's needed, and moves them into unhesitant action—after all, *laws* can only do for you what they can do through you. Even Jesus hinted at this through his teachings on prayer: "Therefore I say unto you, What things soever ye desire, when ye pray, believe that ye receive them, and ye shall have them."[54]

Confronting Our Dark Sides

Because imagination and emotions are key ingredients in using visualization to reach the subconscious mind to overcome undesirable habits, it's of great use to us to become mindful of automatic negative thoughts and emotions.

A part of being human is having a darker side—or, as it's often referred to in the field of psychology, a shadow self. If habits are patterns of being we've adopted to make our lives easier, and emotions are motivating forces driving us to action, a lot of our negative feelings and reactions can likely stem from our shadow selves. Unless there's been significant effort to uncover this part of our personality, the shadow selves reside in the unconscious parts of our awareness. In other words, the shadow self is aspects of character that the conscious mind has refused to accept as part of itself—aspects, for whatever reason, we don't want to admit to having.

According to the great Swiss psychiatrist, Carl Jung, the shadow self is instinctive and irrational and therefore prone to psychological projection. This is when an individual's perceived personal inferiorities are recognized as perceived moral deficiencies in someone else.[55] It is a defense mechanism in which the weaker aspects of our self-image defends itself against repressed desires or qualities by denying their existence in ourselves while attributing them to other people.[56] Basically, projection is when we unconsciously take unwanted emotions or traits we don't like about ourself and attribute them to someone else. For example, when a dishonest person believes others to be deceitful; or when a person who doesn't face their fears begins to see others as cowards; or when a person who's angry all the time sees others as the instigators.

Learning to appreciate and work with the darker sides of our personal natures—which cultivates negative habits—is uncomfortable, but it is necessary. We can start by being honest with ourselves and accepting that those darker sides are indeed within us, and then we can try to understand why they exist. They usually come from some limiting belief or dissatisfaction with the self. By finding quiet time to be one with our own internal dialogs, we can each dig deep and have a counseling session with our Self. By way of this independent therapy session, we'll begin to learn how to view these darker emotions as signals pointing to harmful beliefs or improper attitudes toward aspects of our lives. When we think about it in this light, the things that trigger us into negative thoughts and emotions can be our greatest teachers.

Through this type of introspection, we learn that we cannot hate hatred or be angry at anger; the only way to counteract these forces is to accept them, then respond with their appropriate medicines. For thoughts of hatred, we can find ways to generate empathy and compassion. And any time we think an angry thought, after accepting it as a natural part of our mind, we can immediately begin to reprogram ourselves with thoughts of understanding, harmony, or patience. Since all thoughts and emotions arise from our interpretations, going straight to the source and changing the story we're telling ourselves will dramatically change how we're handling the situation.

Understanding ourselves at our deepest levels takes consistent reflective effort and conscious, rational focus of imagination. It's an endless uncovering of the most important people in our lives: ourselves.

All that's left here is for us to answer the following question:

Are we the type of rider that will let its horse go where it wants, or are we the rider that will work through the hardships and train the stallion to work with us and not against us?

Bestial thoughts crystallize into habits of drunkenness and sensuality, which solidify into circumstances of destitution and disease.

Impure thoughts of every kind crystallize into enervating and confusing habits, which solidify into distracting and adverse circumstances.

Thoughts of fear, doubt, and indecision crystallize into weak, unmanly, and irresolute habits, which solidify into circumstances of failure, indigence, and slavish dependence.

Lazy thoughts crystallize into habits of uncleanliness and dishonesty, which solidify into circumstances of foulness and beggary.

Hateful and condemnatory thoughts crystallize into habits of accusation and violence, which solidify into circumstances of injury and persecution.

Selfish thoughts of all kinds crystallize into habits of self-seeking, which solidify into circumstances more or less distressing.

On the other hand, beautiful thoughts of all kinds crystallize into habits of grace and kindliness, which solidify into genial and sunny circumstances.

Pure thoughts crystallize into habits of temperance and self-control, which solidify into circumstances of repose and peace.

Thoughts of courage, self-reliance, and decision crystallize into manly habits, which solidify into circumstances of success, plenty, and freedom.

Energetic thoughts crystallize into habits of cleanliness and industry, which solidify into circumstances of pleasantness.

Gentle and forgiving thoughts crystallize into habits of gentleness, which solidify into protective and preservative circumstances.

Loving and unselfish thoughts crystallize into habits of self-forgetfulness for others, which solidify into circumstances of sure and abiding prosperity and true riches (Allen).

—As a Man Thinketh, *James Allen*[57]

Our wellbeing is a reflection of how we perceive the world.

▌▌ LIFE WOUNDS

Elder Ting asked Lin-chi, "Master, what is the great meaning of Bud-dha's teachings?"

Lin-chi came down from his seat, slapped Ting, and pushed him away.

Ting was stunned and stood motionless.

A monk nearby said, "Ting, why do you not bow?"

At that moment, Ting attained great enlightenment.[58]

Understanding Our Wounds

In 1969, Bruce Lee received news that would shake his experience of reality and change the course of his life. He had injured his lower back during a routine weightlifting exercise because he hadn't warmed up properly, and his doctors told him that he would never walk normally again. This meant that he had to give up his martial arts practice. However, following the warrior's spirit within, Bruce didn't take this news at face value. Instead, he plunged into studying the nature of his injury and became even more committed to learning about the mind/body connection. To fortify in his mind the idea of his recovery, he took one of his business cards and wrote *walk on* on the back of it, and he carried it with him everywhere he went. Regardless of what his doctors told him, he would *walk on.*

While his body was recuperating, Bruce kept his mind busy. When he was bedridden for a long time, he read and wrote to stay mentally active. In his notes, Bruce wrote,

> Walk on and leave behind all the things that would dam up the inlet or clog the outlet of experience.... You must see clearly what is wrong. You must decide to be cured. Speak so as to aim at being cured. You must act. Your livelihood must not conflict with your therapy. The therapy must go forward at the staying speed. You must feel it and think about it incessantly. And learn how to contemplate with the deep mind.[59]

Most people know Bruce as a fighter; however, Bruce was also a deep thinker. On the surface, it may seem that a fighter's natural inclination is to fight—to resist. Bruce realized that fighting against circumstances would only create more resistance. In other words, he recognized that what happens to an individual isn't necessarily the problem; the problem is a result of how the person reacts to what happens. So instead of fighting what happened—his injury—Bruce accepted circumstances as they were and adapted. He made the best of his situation. His journey to recovery was long and rough, but eventually he created his own path to healing and returned to his practice better than before.

When we think of trauma that completely changes the course of our lives, we often think of the physical injuries that Bruce sustained or the psychological injuries a war veteran might endure, or a combination of both types of injuries, such as with sexual abuse. Not all trauma, however, is a catastrophic occurrence or dramatic life event. In fact, trauma isn't about the event at all; it's about the individual perception of the event—the personal experience of what happened. This is why trauma is much more expansive than most people think. Trauma happens to a person when they encounter any emotional experience that they're not mentally prepared to handle and when they don't have the proper guidance on how to process or work through the emotions in the moment. The person feels threatened and also helpless to change the situation they're in, so they abandon their own needs to cope and stay safe, losing aspects of themselves in the process.

Most of us have experienced trauma, even if the majority of our trauma is overlooked. For instance, as an infant maybe we simply weren't held during a troubling time, or as a child our personal boundaries were somehow violated. Maybe we shared something we created or expressed ourselves in some way, but the endeavor wasn't accepted by others. Times when it seemed we were invisible, unheard, or undervalued often led us to feel loneliness and other overwhelming emotions. These experiences, without adequate care and attention, could have created blockages in our maturation process and stored themselves deep in our memory as traumatic events. Like driving with the emergency brake on, these blockages can be especially bad for people who have experienced more than the average amount of trauma.

When we speak of memory, we often mean images and other sensory observations that the imagination has manufactured, but in the case of trauma, this isn't the complete story. Studies have shown that traumatic stress physically changes the brain,[60] and the stress seeps down into the tissues of the body.[61] Moreover, it alters an individual's perception of reality and causes them to perceive life completely differently than other people do. Referencing the allegory of Plato's cave in chapter two of this book, the shadows on the cave wall are greatly exaggerated, and expectations take over reality. The stories replaying in the mind pollute—and even overwrite, in the case of those with more trauma—what's actually happening.

In a traumatized brain, the individual is in survival mode—the brain is releasing stress hormones into the body to help the person enter fight or flight mode. The rational thinking center and the emotional regulation center are underactive, and the fear center is overactive. Blood pressure increases, muscles tense, and the activity weakens in the parts of the brain that process logical thinking, decision making, and moderation. Now, in a situation where we encounter real danger, this survival mode is not only necessary but critical to preserving our existence. For example, if we're being chased by a bear, it's not important to philosophize with the bear, build a relationship with it, or try to figure out its gender; what's important is that we get to safety. The trouble is, for the traumatized brain, the reflex for this survival mode activation is dysregulated—and it's likely that there's a dependence on the stress hormones that get released.[62]

Recognizing How Our Wounds Affect Us

Living life in survival mode is exhausting. Everything seems to be a challenge. Since our senses are heightened to keep us alert and "safe," our attention is focused on our outer environment—making us, in a literal sense, materialists. This causes a disconnection between the mind and the body's natural intelligence (see chapter six for more information about intuition), and statements such as "Follow your heart" or "Go with your gut" become foreign to us.

As we'll discuss later in the book, the heart and the gut are powerful information processing centers with intelligence and memories of their own; but a person experiencing trauma severs the communicative channels to those parts of themselves. Consequently, the person seems to be dragging themselves through life, confused about who they are and what their life is about. Energy in the form of emotions is trapped in their body, and because the person is scarred from their traumatic experience, they do everything they can to escape those emotions—to escape feeling the buried pain.

This trauma is the cause behind most of the world's drug and alcohol abuse.[63] People try to manage their unbearable situations on their own, and when they find no solution within, they turn outward to their chosen substance. And because this substance provides a sense of relief—essentially helping them cope with their pain—they become much more vulnerable to forming a dependence.

Past trauma may be commonplace in the lives of substance addicts, but an individual who is traumatized will not always become addicted to a specific substance. Escapism can come in many forms, including but not limited to overworking, overeating, hypersexuality, gaming, internet browsing, social media surfing, and anything else that can allow a person to numb themselves to the emotions that arise out of the present moment.

We often shield our trauma, hide it, lie about it, bury it deep within us so that nothing and no one can ever come close to exposing it. It's a desperate attempt to protect ourselves. But why? Usually, it's because of the shame surrounding the experience that initiated the trauma. Since we didn't receive any emotional support during our experience—we didn't have someone to witness or listen to our pain without judging, denying, or embarrassing us—we record the event as something shameful and adopt beliefs aligning with that assessment. The shame of trauma creates a lens through which we see ourselves, other people, and the world around us. We begin to think that we brought the event upon ourselves. We think that we're broken, unworthy, or burdensome to those around us; that we're not good enough the way we are; that no one will love us; and that, eventually, everyone will leave us. We find it difficult to trust others because we don't trust ourselves, but we still feel like we need someone to rescue, save, or fix us. Sometimes we don't feel safe in our own body, we view the world as unfair, and we believe that life is destined to be a never-ending struggle. In adverse cases, we may even believe that we deserve to be hurt—a belief that can lead to addiction and self-harm. Shame tells us that we don't deserve joy, success, or fulfillment; it makes us believe that we deserve to be used by others, that our own needs should be ignored. As a result, when we're traumatized we become isolated and locked up in our own misery. Then we attract and build bonds with people who are ashamed like us, further reinforcing the self-image of *the victim*.

Victims of trauma are recognizable because they're often on extreme ends. They're either too alert (overreactive to the slightest touch) or too numb (heavy, sluggish, and immobile). In environments where they're interacting with others, they experience chronic social anxiety; they constantly compare themselves with others and get stuck in loops of self-judgment. They have an obsessive desire to be chosen by others and are hypervigilant about what others think of them. In their relationships, they're always worrying about whether they're liked and wanted, whether they said the right thing, etc. When it comes to their goals and aspirations, they procrastinate, doubt their abilities, and self-sabotage.

Because trauma victims are in survival mode, they're not as receptive to natural signs and signals. Their reticular activating system isn't tuned correctly to pick up on the pathways to progress—to the achievement of their goals. Instead, it's tuned to trigger the same traumatic stories to replay over and over in their minds. While these people are wired for success deep down, they have faulty connections trapping energy, keeping it from flowing freely.

People who suffer emotionally from trauma don't only suffer in their minds though. Because trauma gets stored in the body, symptoms also show up in their bodies—in the way they sit, stand, breathe, walk; in their posture, their sleep patterns, their digestion, their diet; in their attitudes toward exercise and meditation; and in how they treat themselves overall.

Living with trauma is like walking with weights around your ankles. It's disadvantageous to growth in any aspect of life. Avoiding or prolonging facing buried pain generally leads to more suffering later, and eventually, a fixed mindset about life.

Healing is possible though. Because the brain is ever changing (see chapter nine for information about neuroplasticity), trauma can be reversed. The discoveries of science and philosophy assure us that no traumatized individual is ever beyond rescue. As long as there's life within, it's never too late; recovery is possible.

Perceiving Our Wounds

We have the ability to heal from trauma because trauma is not the truth of who we are. It is merely a perspective of who we are based on past events in our lives. It's a part in the ever-unfolding story; and really, when taken into consideration, it's just a small part of the story—a small, malleable part.

Consider that this small yet exaggerated part in our story could even be essential for our ability to become the people we need to be

in order to achieve our greatest desires. This may seem like a radical idea at first, since traumatic events are so intimate, but studies show that more than half of all trauma survivors report positive changes and never-expected growth in their lives thanks to the incidents.[64] It's stated that people who experienced traumatic events display more positive change than people who have never had an extraordinarily difficult event in their lives. In particular, the changes include seeing new possibilities, relating to others, increasing personal strength, changing spiritually, and appreciating life. Those coping with the aftermath of trauma who have higher scores in these areas are determined to be more successful in reconstructing and strengthening their perceptions of self, others, and the meaning of events.[65]

Could we, in the midst of navigating and trying to understand an emotionally shocking experience, be subject to having a limited view?

For an example of how quickly and easily we can jump to conclusions about the meaning of something, consider the different points of view we get when we change the level of magnification on any object. We can look at something with a microscope, then look at it with the naked eye, and then again with a telescope. In each case, we would see the same object differently, and because of that, we would come to different conclusions about what we're seeing. However, it wouldn't be accurate to say that one magnification level is more correct than the other; they're all the same object, just different points of view. To illustrate further, imagine a portrait painting. With the naked eye, we'd see a person, but if we digitally uploaded this painting onto a computer and zoomed in, we would begin to see small, randomly colored dots scattered throughout the screen. It would be impossible to make out what the original image was at this level of magnification; all the dots would seem meaningless, separate, and disconnected from each other. However, as we slowly zoomed back out, we'd begin to see a pattern. Then, zooming out some more, this pattern—which was once a seemingly meaningless collection of dots—would suddenly make sense as it rearranged itself into a person again.

Medical practitioners are familiar with this idea of inspecting things from different points of view before forming conclusions. When they examine our blood streams under a microscope, they see an all-out war between all sorts of microorganisms. Taking a narrow-minded view, one might mistake this fight to the death between the cells in the human body as a sign of ill-health or disease. However, in reality, the wellbeing of our entire organism depends on the continuance of this fight; it's a sign of a healthy, properly functioning immune system. In other words, what the medical practitioner sees with the degree of magnification from the microscope is conflict, war, torture, and trauma. Yet, with a higher view of things, the practitioner can acknowledge the harmony, balance, and wholesomeness.

From these examples, we can begin to understand that our view of ourselves and our life events is just a view from a particular magnification of consciousness. Our level of awareness, especially with such an intimate traumatizing event, may be lacking. However, if we could find a way to take the seemingly meaningless, separate, and disconnected conflicts, struggles, and sufferings of our lives and change the level of magnification, we may find that we might make some sense of it.

This "making some sense of it," however, would not be possible if we continue to bury or ignore our pains and problems.

Deciding to Be Healthy

A person needs to make the decision to be healthy, but the term *to make a decision* is not to be taken lightly. *Decision* is a Latin word that means "to cut off." *Making a decision* literally means cutting off all other choices and focusing on one. The act of deciding is a liberating one because it frees a person from having to consider all the endless choices that are available to them. When an individual decides on something, they now have a goal in mind—a vision of what's possible. This vision gives a person something to show up for, an ideal to reach. It gives them something new to welcome into their life—a possibility in the unknown they're willfully stepping into.

There are three choices an individual needs to make daily to maintain health: the choice of the healthier alternative, the choice to follow through, the choice to welcome something new. But because of how the brain functions, knowing which choice to make and making it don't always coincide. As expressed in previous chapters, the mind operates like a muscle. Those just beginning to train this muscle again will need to commit to follow through until they completely reprogram their mental blueprint and take back control of the six mental faculties (willpower, imagination, reasoning, memory, perception, intuition). There are numerous techniques and methods for this, but essentially the regimen a person decides to develop must incorporate these three qualities: altered state of mind, connection to community, and self-directed change through goals.

Altered States of Mind

Welcoming the new can make all the difference for someone who has been stuck replaying the same patterns. It's the objective that hypnotherapy seeks to accomplish with the patient: to access different brain states, creating a type of focused attention and increased suggestibility to help the person envision new possibilities for themselves. A healthy person goes through all of these states naturally, but for people who have experienced great trauma, it becomes harder to access the different states. However, a traumatized person can access these brain states through various means, not just through hypnotherapy.

To access the brain wave states, the person must first feel safe and at ease. They can do this with the help of some breathing techniques or even just connecting with a person they trust or a pet. When the person feels safe and relaxed, they leave the beta brain wave state, which has the individual focused on the external world (cognitive tasks, threats, happenings in the environment), and enter the alpha brain wave state. In the alpha brain wave state, the individual is more relaxed and centered in the present moment; they are calm in their inner world of thoughts and emotions yet alert to what is happening around them. In this state, the individual can absorb new information better, and they also have enhanced mental coordination and greater mind/body integration. Alpha brain waves play a key role in healthy brain activity—particularly with reducing symptoms of depression and anxiety.

Most importantly, though, the alpha brain wave state is the bridge into the next-level brain wave state, where the suggestions made to the subconscious can have a greater impact: theta. In the theta brain wave state, the doors to the subconscious are wide open, and there's a gateway into learning, memory, intuition, and, most notably, the self-image. This is the programmable state a child is in up until about the age of seven. It's where the individual's attention withdraws from the external environment and focuses on the inner world—focuses on assigning meaning to what's happening. It's the twilight state accessed right after waking up and right before falling asleep, and also during deep meditation. In the theta brain wave state, the individual can expand their horizons and see the abundance of options that are available to them. This state permits massive shifts out of the victim consciousness caused by trauma and into a mindset of empowerment.

Yet, there's still another state that the brain enters where even greater recovery occurs: the delta brain wave state. The delta state is usually accessed during deep, restorative sleep. However, an individual who has the practice of going deep in their meditations can also access the delta brain wave state. In this state, external awareness is completely suspended, and an individual's attention is centered solely upon the inner world for healing and regeneration. When a person enters this state through meditation, their body experiences what it would during deep sleep, but their mind is still awake—their brain processes extraordinarily high amplitudes of energy. As a result, there are opportunities to access a state of *cosmic consciousness* and have profound mystical experiences—like the feeling of one-ness discussed in chapter one: feeling connected to everyone and everything in the universe. Just one of these mystical experiences is powerful enough to trigger recovery from even the most extreme traumatic events.

Welcoming the new into our lives involves accepting the idea of letting go of the known to step into the unknown. It asks a person to surrender—or grow out of—the old identity they've formed and instead invite a future that is filled with new possibilities and poten-tial. Among the simplest and most profound ways to initiate this process is through meditation, which we discuss in chapter seven.

Connection to Community

Since our wellbeing is a reflection of how we perceive the world, our greatest wounds would be connected to how we view ourselves, other people, and the meanings we assign to the happenings of life. This idea is reflected in Maslow's hierarchy of psychological health needs (as discussed in chapter six), particularly in the stages of *love and belonging* and *esteem*. The link is clear; improving mental health involves having healthy attitudes about family life and social life—environments that traumatized people have considerable narrative around.

The story repeating in the mind of an individual who has expe-rienced trauma is often one in which they play the role of a victim of circumstances—a powerless, broken victim. The mental blueprint they're operating from doesn't include a strong sense of self-worth or inner security. Because of their perception, relating to others in a fulfilling way is challenging. Many of their relationships have formed from a place of lack, based strictly on fulfilling personal needs. In other words, relationships are a place they go to get something, rather than to give, share, and relate.

This misperception is justified in the mind of a traumatized individual because they believe this is simply the nature of human beings. Because of their life experiences and all the times they feel they've let themselves down, they find it difficult to trust themselves and, as a result, to trust others. People suffering from past trauma often don't feel like they fit in, and they don't feel like they can express themselves honestly and be accepted. Instead, they feel alienated from others—there's a lack of belonging in any group or community. This causes them to sometimes repel others with their communication and behavior without even realizing it, and then they feel even more isolated and lonely. The neurological element taking place within the traumatized person's brain wiring that keeps them stuck in a stress-response mode is often unrecognized by the victim. This makes them react to everyday events as though they're constantly reliving their trauma.

What a traumatized individual needs in order to overcome isolation is to first recognize how their trauma is affecting their life and relationships. With a certain degree of awareness, the person can begin to acknowledge how the narrative in their mind externalizes as life events and experiences. The continuous chain of negative thoughts about ourselves and others doesn't stay in the mind; it eventually manifests itself in behavior and leaks into relationships. Without first understanding the ways our views affect ourselves and others, it's difficult to accept the need to rewrite the mental script so that we can have healthy interpersonal bonds.

This is why healing is usually achieved in communal settings and with the help of others who have shared values. Not only is the social support and feeling of community vital, but because the trauma we experience usually happens around other human beings, it's only natural that our recovery process include human beings as well. Social wellness depends on communicating constructively, experiencing care and support, and feeling like we're a part of something. That's what community is about: connection. It's not just a group of people who come together and form a club or a team—it's a feeling of connection with others, of being accepted for who we are. This connection makes us feel safe, wanted, and loved, and it also gives us a sense of purpose through the roles we take on in the community. Having purpose—feeling like we're useful—and being there for others help give meaning to life.

The goal of healing is to feel fully alive. And to be alive as a human being—a social creature—means to live harmoniously with other human beings.

Self-Directed Change through Goals

The human being is a being who strives toward goals. Because of this, setting goals is an important step to recovering from trauma and poor mental health. Working toward specific goals can help an individual get closer to the life they want while learning to manage their pain from the past. This principle ties in intimately with the fourth stage of Maslow's hierarchy of psychological health needs: *esteem*.

Striving for accomplishments and overcoming challenges is critical to building healthy self-esteem and increasing confidence. By being motivated to compete, perform, and make our mark, we stretch ourselves toward individual freedom and self-expression. Not only does aspiring to achieve specific goals help us recognize our strengths, but it helps us gain respect—both from ourselves and from others.

Goals are ideal circumstances to aim at. By setting a goal, we acknowledge that there's a discrepancy between our desired situation and our current reality—our ideal self and our actual self. When we understand this discrepancy, it's a powerful motivating force. We are motivated to close the gap between our present-day situations and our ideal circumstances by attempting to realize our ideal selves. By taking gradual steps forward toward our goals, we slowly change our circumstances. Each step forward reinforces positive belief structures and encourages us to invest even more effort. Not only do we get closer to the life we want, but we simultaneously crawl out of the victim mentality and develop a healthy self-image.

Practically everybody has goals and aspirations in their life; however, many people fail to reach their aims not because of a lack of intelligence or courage but because they don't organize their mental faculties around the goal. The proper way to set goals is using the S.M.A.R.T. approach—a method first described by a consultant and strategic planner named George T. Doran in his paper "There's a S.M.A.R.T. Way to Write Management's Goals and Objectives."[66] Below are the five criteria of S.M.A.R.T. goals:

Specific: Goals must be clearly defined. The goal should include who is involved, what will be accomplished, where it will be done, and why it's important. Instead of creating a goal to just "exercise more," include some more details, such as "I will jog for fifteen minutes at the park five days of the week to improve physical health and emotional wellbeing."

Measurable: Goals must be created in a way that's easy to measure. Answering the questions of "how many" or "how much" allows a person to track progress and measure outcomes. For instance, instead of having a goal to "drink more water," modify it to "drink two liters of water per day." This will provide valuable data that an individual can use to prove progress or reevaluate when necessary.

Achievable: Goals must challenge a person to step out of their comfort zones, but the goals should be realistic. The best goals are neither too easy nor too difficult. Suppose that someone wants to lose weight. Setting a goal to drop 100 lbs. in one month does not follow the S.M.A.R.T. guidelines. All goals should be reasonable and attainable within a certain timeframe so that the person can stay focused and motivated to achieve them.

Relevant: Goals must be worthwhile, important, and beneficial. They should align with a person's greater desires and overall vision, and the results should make a difference in the individual's life. If a goal doesn't align with values and long-term objectives, the individual probably needs to rethink it. For example, if a person aspires to become the greatest BBQ chef in their state, it wouldn't be much use to them to spend their time learning about international vegetarian cuisine.

Time-Based: It's been said that a goal without a plan and a deadline is just a wish. Goals must have realistic end-dates so that a person can effectively prioritize and manage daily or weekly tasks. Deadlines keep people motivated and engaged. Let's say a person is just starting out in real estate and wants to grow their business to produce a yearly six-figure income. It would be beneficial to have an ideal date they would like to produce this income by so that they can formulate an effective plan to make it happen. Otherwise, it's very likely tasks would get put off and procrastination would get the best of them.

To help you decide on some goals to set, think about what's important to you. What are your hopes and dreams? What do you enjoy doing and would like to do more? What are some areas of your life that you'd like to improve? What will it take for you to feel free or happy in your life?

Then, once you have a goal in mind, you can ask yourself this question every day: "What is one thing I can do today that will help me bridge the gap between where I am and where I want to be?"

No matter where an individual is on their mental health journey, they can always set goals and work toward them. Those with more trauma and who struggle with mental health should start small. When it comes to new endeavors, everybody starts from the bottom, and there's no shame in being a beginner. As John Pierpont Morgan, one of the world's wealthiest and most successful businessmen, once said, "The first step towards getting somewhere is to decide you're not going to stay where you are."

Doing what we've always done will inevitably give us what we've always gotten. That's what validates the power behind decisions: they shape our destiny. We're always one decision away from a new life.

To recover from trauma, we must decide to detox from our past and rewrite the narrative in our minds. Our stories aren't fixed, and neither are our memories. We can choose to remember differently, and we can choose to change the meaning of what happened. We can begin to reprogram our minds to feel differently about ourselves and about what happened. This recovery is attainable when we change the magnification level through which we view our past circumstances, enter a relaxed state of mind to influence the subconscious, communicate our past and pain with others, and work toward a desirable future.

Going Through to Get Out

In the case of trauma, though, in spite of our best efforts, recovery doesn't end with matters of the mind—with a change of the story. The body also remembers. The only way out of the pain is through it, and the only way through it is by using both the body and the mind. Because healing entails reconnecting with the body, taking the body more seriously will allow the recovery that leads to emotional wellness.

Disconnecting from mental chatter and being mindful are critical factors in recovery. Getting inside one's own body, relaxing, and feeling sensations without worrying about threats are key experiences an individual needs in order to heal. A person must calmly acknowledge and accept the feelings, thoughts, and bodily sensations that arise from the present moment. In most cases, the person will find themselves facing uncomfortable emotional circumstances, and it's at this moment that they will be most tempted to escape, bury the feeling, or numb themselves. This is where self-compassion plays a major role. The individual must find a way to genuinely accept their circumstances regardless of what they discover about themselves from within. To do this, they must experience all the emotions that arise out of the moment and recognize them for what they are: temporary states of mind stemming from one's circumstances and mood. Then, to release the feelings, the person must consciously breathe through them. This is the act of *letting go*, and it's the path to creating inner peace.

To aid in this transformative process, there are countless disciplines, hobbies, and practices. Martial arts and yoga are the predominant ones with the most scientific research behind them, but other practices such as swimming, breathwork, running, singing, dancing, gymnastics, and acrobatics have been known to help as well. The idea is for an individual to become involved in an activity that can help them release pent-up emotions and honestly express themselves through both body and mind. Most of these practices also provide a community to connect to and receive social support from, and they also challenge an individual on multiple levels to refine not only the physical aspects of their nature but also the mental aspects—to become stronger, more agile, more flexible, and more emotionally stable.

It's imperative to keep in mind that the meditative aspects of these disciplines are just as crucial to recovery as the physical aspects. Meditation and exercise are *critical* to one's wellbeing and should be taken as seriously as food, sleep, and hygiene. We wouldn't skip a meal or a night of sleep because we "don't feel like it," so we shouldn't skip the practices of exercise and meditation if we truly want a great quality of life. Such a life is available to each of us, and, by our birthright, we deserve it.

If trauma is a disconnection from our authentic self—from feeling unsafe and foreign in our own bodies—then healing is the reconnection to it. Recovery from any sort of traumatic event is possible, but the traumatized individual needs to *decide* to recover. They need to follow through with their decision, get the help that's required, and welcome and accept any internal experience necessary for the sake of their treatment.

When we understand the variety of options available to us, we begin to recognize how our healing and recovery is in our own hands. By confronting our pain and learning to view our circumstances with the level of magnification that suits us best, we allow ourselves to make sense of our suffering. It's in the process of studying our individual experiences and learning about the mind/body connection that we discover our own path, that we recognize the need to *walk on* toward healing. To aid us on this path, there are several practices with dozens of methods and techniques, but it's up to each person to discover the one that fits them best—the one that helps them find union and wholeness within.

Ultimately, the path of healing teaches an individual what it means to be a human being. But even more, it teaches that it's okay to be *this* human being.

"Not the world, not what's outside of us, but what we hold inside traps us. We may not be responsible for the world that created our minds, but we can take responsibility for the mind with which we create our world." —Gabor Maté

Our ability to shift our perspectives may be the single most powerful and effective method for us to become the people we need to be.

12 BUILDING CHANGE

"Suzuki Roshi, I've been listening to your lectures for years," a student
said during the question and answer time following a lecture, *"but I just
don't understand. Could you just please put it in a nutshell? Can you
reduce Buddhism to one phrase?"*

Everyone laughed. Suzuki laughed.

"Everything changes," he said. *Then he asked for another question.*[67]

The Need to Adapt

Through meditation, personal reflection, cognitive reframing,
and visualization, we can realize our ability to reprogram our subconscious mind to heal from the past, enjoy the present, and align
ourselves closer to the future we desire. Naturally, we might face
some resistance in the beginning, as with any shift into an unfa-
miliar experience. This might make us feel uncomfortable for a
little while. It is probable that we'll grieve a past version of our *self*
when going through a big change. We experience this discomfort
because the settled self-image—the soon to be past self—feels it's
in danger of death; and, in a sense, it is. We're basically killing parts
of ourselves to transcend into new people—retiring familiar ways
of thinking and behaving for different ones. So, this part of our

self (the idea of who we are) which feels threatened opposes the changes. This discomfort is merely the ego's attempt at discouraging us from making the lifestyle adjustments we want; it always wants to stay with what's familiar, with what it's used to.

Nevertheless, through correct mental preparation, we can better prepare ourselves for our spar with the ego. By voluntarily confronting that which we feel a resistance to—that which frightens us but will bring us closer to our desires—we put ourselves in a position where we can exercise and strengthen our mental faculties (imagination, will, intuition, perception, memory, and reason) and reorganize ourselves for the inevitable discomfort that is part of growth. However, if we don't acknowledge and overcome the discomfort, the momentum of our habitual previous self will hold us in the same patterns, and we'll continue to manifest the same types of problems; consequently, we'll reinforce the same underdeveloped self-image.

Clinging onto the same patterns can become a problem because if it continues long enough, we're inclined to attach ourselves to that underdeveloped self-image. Going forward, the more we reject our need for change, thinking, "This is who I am," the more we'll suffer from feelings of being stuck, like pushing a boulder uphill—which is really just a condition of not being true to our higher Self, to the warrior's spirit within us.

We've discussed the importance of courage to face our circumstances and to become self-sufficient. However, prior to courage, we need acceptance of change and willingness to change. We must accept the fact that in life we experience change and that it's totally natural—in fact, beneficial and necessary. Change is the one thing we can always depend on. All things change; our relationships, our bodies, our emotions, even nature itself. The pleasures we feel today can be pains we feel tomorrow. As John Henry Newman said, "To live is to change, and to be perfect is to have changed often."[68] If we resist, we just make things more difficult on ourselves. The moment we accept and flow with change, we'll become more empowered to deal with all of life's situations.

We accept change and counter resistance by acknowledging our true needs. When we acknowledge the fact that outside our basic needs for food, clothing, and shelter, we don't need much, we put ourselves in a state to accept life's changes. Eastern philosophies call this state "nonattachment." It means "deep involvement in life—because there is a lack of attachment to the outcome."[69] This is especially true for the entrepreneur with massive goals as it shifts their view from looking into the future to being completely present to find enjoyment in the process.

We shouldn't get lost in the idea that we need external things such as money, fame, success, or even perfect health. Everything that we need is in our minds. We simply need to turn our focus inward and explore.

After accepting that the mind—including our awareness over the mind—is of the highest importance to our lives and wellbeing, we can learn to identify mental states—thoughts, feelings, and attitudes—that will help us develop ourselves further. With our focus inward, we'll find characteristics of a positive nature and things of a negative nature. During our exploration, we'll learn to recognize constructive and harmful mental states and then we can plan to increase and decrease accordingly. For example, if we want good health and happiness for ourselves, we can find all the inner causes that increase the state of mind that produces good health and happiness and those that decrease health and happiness. Once we identify the various behaviors and states, we can remove the negative causes and feed the positive ones. By finding time to reflect on our activities and involvements, and the mental states that they produce, we can recognize what's working for us and what's working against us.

Awareness and Resistance

Typically, there will be an inclination to begin labeling these various activities as either positive or negative, and we should be wary of that. We shouldn't label any activity "good" or "bad" because they're all natural—*good* for some things and *bad* for others. It's up to each of us to categorize them based on whether they allow us to progress toward our goals. If we see that the emotions or thoughts produced from an activity is detrimental toward our objectives, we try to understand and avoid it. Likewise, if we find the opposite to be true, we strive to create more of those thoughts and emotions.

Sometimes previously categorized positive states of mind may turn out to later produce negatively categorized behaviors. This is where the state of nonattachment becomes increasingly useful. By not being attached to certain ways of being and doing, we can regularly make adjustments with less effort—and we should, because life is constantly making its own adjustments. Just as the seasons change and a fruit tree lets go of its leaves and fruits, if we want to be quick to adapt, we must be willing to let go of certain views and ideas. By investing attention into identifying which behaviors and states serve our current conditions, we bring awareness to what's necessary for the next stage of our development. And because the ego will always rationalize a need for a negative habit, thinking pattern, or emotion, it's in this very same awareness that change can begin to take place. In this sense, there's an unceasing encounter between awareness and resistance where ego attempts to conceal our shortcomings.

We can draw a brilliant illustration about this internal fight from a popular folktale: Imagine two wolves live inside each of us, locked in a never-ending battle. One wolf symbolizes evil, ego, or fear. It's filled with hatred, anger, envy, greed, false pride, laziness, guilt, and dishonesty. This wolf leads a meager and miserable life and believes that the world is cruel and unpleasant, and there's not enough to go around. For this negatively charged wolf, other people are mostly bad, and it's either kill or be killed.

Then there's the other wolf, which symbolizes virtue, spirit, or love. This wolf is filled with peace, joy, kindness, humility, empathy, generosity, compassion, and truth. It has a positive attitude and acts with certainty; it has faith that it can accomplish anything. This wolf lives a life of abundance, and it believes creation is ultimately pleasant and giving.

When hearing about these opposite characteristics, we might wonder which wolf is stronger. The folktale has a simple answer for this inquiry: "The one we choose to feed."

We humans will always be susceptible to worry, anger, and frustration. However, if we've fed the positive-natured wolf by redirecting our thoughts to more productive ends, we can handle those negative states and they will pass more easily. Within us is the strength to keep those negative experiences from seeping deeper into us and intensifying, becoming ingrained in our psyche. Resistance and discomfort can instead come and just pass through us, without creating additional suffering. His Holiness the Dalai Lama has a great expression for this idea in his book *Ethics for the New Millennium*: "A moment of sorrow does not become disabling grief unless we hold on to it and add negative thoughts and imaginings."[70]

Cultivating this state of mind is not about suppressing or denying negative thoughts and emotions. That may seem like a great short-term solution, but it would actually be an incredible waste of energy. Denial and repression only make the process of change harder over time. Therefore, effort shouldn't be placed in controlling the mind and its behaviors but liberating it. When the mind is liberated, thoughts come and go spontaneously; nothing is held onto. The process is more about observation and the rational understanding of the destructive nature of these so-called negative states of mind. Whether of positive nature or negative, we are not our thoughts. Our thoughts are just passing events in the mind. With a voluntary and deliberate effort to understand all aspects of ourselves—our thoughts, emotions, attitudes, behaviors and our impact on our environment—we work to dissolve any false ideals of ourselves and of others. This leads to acceptance, which gives us insight as to where our energies should be applied.

The Habit of Self-Discipline

It takes discipline to overcome our own negative qualities; however, we know we're making progress if we notice changes in our behavior, changes that ultimately bring us closer to others and closer to our goals. It's easier to do what's most convenient, but sometimes what's most convenient isn't the best for others—or even ourselves. Therefore, it can be said that ethical behavior is a mark of inner self-discipline. Think about when the water in a lake is stirred up by a storm. The mud from the lake's bottom begins to cloud the water. However, the nature of the water isn't dirty, so when the storm passes and the mud settles, the water is left clear again. This is a metaphor for how the mind works when flushed with negative thoughts and emotions. Sometimes, especially when we're riled up, we can be shortsighted in how we react to life's events. We want to be calm and levelheaded when responding so that our acts are beneficial to circumstances. It takes self-discipline to wait until we're in such a state—to wait until the storm passes and the water is clear. By having wholesome motivations for our words and actions, it's more likely that we'll contribute to situations and the wellbeing of others.

Achieving this type of inner discipline is possible because of how our brains are designed. We are adaptable beings. Our brains are wired with instinctual behavior patterns to help us respond to and survive in any environment. The brain designs new patterns, cells, and neurotransmitters in response to the new input it receives. (See chapter nine for a more detailed discussion of this process, called *neuroplasticity*.) So because new thoughts and fresh perspectives can reshape the ways our brain cells work, it's entirely possible to realign our circumstances to a greater good.

Self-transformation, however, requires self-awareness as well as self-discipline. If we have self-awareness, we know our current capabilities and where we stand. We know what we're good at and where we come up short. We know how to treat people and we don't try to be something we're not because we understand that our behavior has consequences. Most importantly, we know what we want. Self-discipline is a requirement as well because we need to be able to do something we're not good at until we get good at it. If we can't stand it when things are perceived as difficult, we'll never become good at anything useful. Moreover, it will be difficult to build the self-esteem to set aside the opinions of others—the outside noise— and focus on what needs our attention. However, with the intention to build self-awareness and self-discipline, it's entirely possible to transform ourselves. We initiate this process by providing new input to the brain—by learning and changing our views.

Our ability to shift our perspectives may be the single most powerful and effective method for us to become the people we need to be and to create the lives we want. All each of us needs is a new approach to each of the problems we face. For instance, we can be disappointed about being laid off from work, or we can become excited about new employment opportunities. We can become upset about being evicted and forced to move, or we can look forward to creating a new home in a new place. We can be unhappy about relationships that didn't work out, or we can become eager to develop ourselves so that we can enter the next relationships in better, more stable states.

The Flexible Mind

When we become obsessed with the problems at hand, we can see only the problems. We become self-absorbed and view those problems as bigger than they really are. This is the irrational habit many of us have when faced with any significant challenge.

It's easy to become obsessed with our problems as our minds see them, consistently replaying the difficulties. To shrink a problem down to its actual size, it helps to remain thankful that it wasn't worse, and that people have overcome such situations before. This gratitude-seeking perspective makes life's troubles much less disturbing and much more manageable.

Our tendency to see only the negative is formed entirely through our own perspectives. We can combat this tendency to see only the negative by approaching all situations with a suspension of judgement, as if good and bad didn't exist. (This method is illustrated in a great story in the next chapter.) This allows us to entertain different ideas and outlooks simultaneously. If we can cultivate open minds and see things from different interpretations, we give ourselves opportunities to view situations in their entirety. The big pictures and small pictures both can become available to us, but only if we allow them.

If we view scenarios from different perspectives, we'll be able to separate significant details from insignificant ones—the worthwhile from the meaningless. This ability will help us achieve our goals, but it will also help us survive. The species that survive longest are the ones that are most adaptable to change.[71] This is true not just in evolution but in all areas of life, including business.

During times of sudden and unexpected changes, being fully present to make fruitful decisions requires us to have flexibility in thinking. Flexible minds equip us to manage not only changes but also the internal pressures that arise because of changes. If we fail to discipline our minds into flexibility, we go on developing worldviews characterized by misunderstanding. With flexible minds, though, we can thrive in even the most hectic of situations, and we can build better connections with other people through understanding.

Self-awareness, inner discipline, and flexibility in our thinking are the qualities that cultivate positive perspectives, and these perspectives allow for growth, fulfillment, and peace of mind—regardless of any changes we experience.

"Empty your mind. Be formless, shapeless—like water. If you put water into a cup, it becomes the cup. You put water into a bottle, it becomes the bottle. You put it in a teapot, it becomes the teapot. Now, water can flow or it can crash. Be water, my friend." —*Bruce Lee*

During periods when we find ourselves miserable, we should stop trying to not be so miserable.

13 FINDING COMFORT IN THE UNCOMFORTABLE

The lobster's a soft, mushy animal that lives inside of a rigid shell. That rigid shell does not expand.

How can the lobster grow? Well, as the lobster grows, that shell becomes very confining, and the lobster feels itself under pressure and uncomfortable. It goes under a rock formation to protect itself from predatory fish, casts off the shell, and produces a new one. Well, eventually, that shell becomes very uncomfortable as it grows. Back under the rocks. The lobster repeats this numerous times.

The stimulus for the lobster to be able to grow is that it feels uncomfortable. Now, if lobsters had doctors, they would never grow because as soon as the lobster feels uncomfortable, it goes to the doctor, gets a Valium, gets a Percocet, feels fine, never casts off his shell.

I think that we have to realize that times of stress are also times that are signals for growth, and if we use adversity properly, we can grow through adversity.

—Rabbi Dr. Abraham Twerski[72]

The Inevitability of Discomfort

From our research today, there are two main differences between humans and other animal species on our planet: our ability of complex reasoning and our use of complex language. These capabilities allow us to choose what situations mean to us and how we respond to them—which can either help us solve or create difficult problems in our lives.

The universe acts in many different ways for many different individuals. We're not always going to be enthusiastic about what we must deal with. Regardless of how much we apply ourselves, there's just some things we cannot change. What we *can* do is change how we interpret situations; and we start by assuming responsibility over our circumstances. For example, the next time you think someone is being unkind, consider that they may be having a horrible day (or life). Sometimes a person's upbringing is radically different from that which you expect; certain mishaps and traumas could cause a person to have trouble with social encounters. People may just be ignorant to the impact they have on others' emotions. Along the same lines, not everyone who doubts your ability to reach a goal thinks small of you; they may actually be lacking self-confidence and simply be projecting their insecurities onto others—really, they think small of themselves. The general theme of this idea is not to take life's perceived misfortunes personally, but to still hold yourself accountable to your views.

The only rational thing to do is to accept the nature of others and the nature of the universe and to assume responsibility for ourselves—to focus on what we can control: what we focus on, what things mean to us, and what we'll do. Such acceptance is a necessity, even if it means facing an uncomfortable truth: in life, there is suffering.

Having awareness of the human condition doesn't make it any easier to accept. We know suffering and failing are a part of life. We know no one is singled out for misfortune. Yet, we still experience the discomfort that accompanies trying situations; this is necessary for the growth of every being in nature.

To better deal with life's trials and to fortify peace in our mind, it helps to realize that mental discomfort and suffering are not things we need to fear or reject. Instead, they should be accepted as natural parts of life, parts we must learn to work through.

The reality is, we have a lot more power than we think we do; most of us just have a habit of letting our rational minds work against us instead of for us—which in turn transforms slight discomforts into great suffering. For instance, we can look inward and explore the feelings of anxiety and excitement. These two emotions are so closely related that brain scans show the same area of the brain lighting up on either emotion.[73] Hence, with a single shift in perspective, we can go from experiencing nervousness to enthusiasm by changing our language around the emotion. As an example, imagine a rollercoaster ride: as the cart climbs up, people could be laughing and yelling from exhilaration, looking forward to the drop they'll experience, or they could be uneasy and in a state of complete apprehension, gripping the safety bars or punching the seat in front of them. Some discomfort might be inevitable, but when it comes down to it, no one else is in charge of what goes on in our minds. It's up to us to define each situation and its meaning to us—otherwise, one will be automatically assigned for us, generally working against us.

The Three Poisons

In Buddhist teachings, the "three poisons of the mind" are the roots of suffering. The poisons are ignorance (defined as a fundamental misunderstanding of the true nature of life), attachment, and aversion (hatred).[74] Buddhists believe suffering is in our nature and that we can't avoid life's tough situations. However, they also believe that accepting these truths and keeping our minds free from the three poisons can put the unavoidable troubles of life in the right mental context, allowing us to avoid further suffering.[75] With a patient and self-compassionate approach, not only can we face any discomfort, we can also turn every trial into an opportunity. This kind of perspective helps us develop mindsets that can end unnecessary suffering.

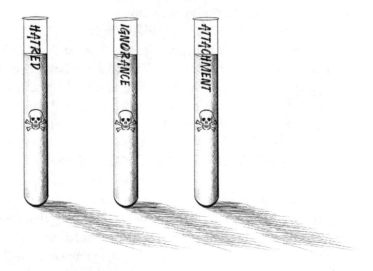

The trouble with the human mind is that it can adapt to live with the three poisons, consequently developing self-deceptive but powerful strategies to avoid dealing with the pain or discomfort that will neutralize the toxicity within. Our methods for avoiding discomfort range from denying a problem's existence (possibly projecting it onto others), to obsessing over television, social media, video games, food, technology, sex, or drugs. There's nothing wrong with these devices and activities in and of themselves but they're not productive uses of time and using them as an escape from our situations can end up causing greater pain/discomfort down the road. The temporary highs we receive can distract us from our troubles for a while, but eventually the pleasure subsides; we build tolerance in the form of desensitization. Then we not only have to face the issues we were trying to avoid, we also have to deal with the serious social, emotional, physical, and mental damages that cause far more suffering than the original problems. These patterns of avoiding discomfort generally leads to years of unhappiness and bitterness.

The Buddhists have the right idea about accepting suffering as a natural part of human life but also about remaining open to the possibility of freedom from suffering—completely curing the three poisons. This view permits tolerance in the form of patience, and it prepares us to face issues head on. When we don't avoid thinking about upsetting problems, we allow the natural wiring in our brain to make the necessary connections it needs to deal with it. This discipline makes it so that we're always in a better position to understand the problems at hand and what we can do about them.

Of course, mentally preparing for troubles does not ease them, but it certainly gives us the strength to cope with them. Acceptance helps us uncover deeper meanings to our suffering so that we can be better geared to endure it. During periods when we find ourselves miserable, we should stop trying to not be so miserable. Instead, we should consider another point of view. Understanding the significance of our troubles can give us a higher tolerance toward suffering and can counteract the feelings of dissatisfaction and sadness. *Understanding* is the road through the pain.

The other option is to deny our pain, resist the changes, and adopt the victim mentality ("Why me?"). This choice only prolongs our suffering and adds to the pressure and discomfort we'll inevitably experience. This way of rejecting uncomfortable circumstances leads to the tendency to imprison ourselves in our own minds. It causes us to narrow our perspectives by misinterpreting everything that happens in terms of its immediate effect on us, as if we're the center of the world. To better deal with life's trials and get closer to real peace of mind, we must realize that discomfort and suffering are not something to be feared or rejected; rather, they're to be accepted and viewed as a natural part of life and growth.

Through the Troubles

Once upon a time, there was a wise Chinese farmer who had a break in the fence surrounding his farm. One of his horses noticed and ran away.

All his neighbors came around that evening and expressed their sympathies; they said it was too bad, and it was an unlucky situation for him to be in.

Unfazed, the farmer smiled and said, "Maybe."

The next day the farmer's horse returned to the farm with three wild horses.

Shortly after, all the neighbors came around and told the farmer how lucky he was and that it was a great position to be in.

Unfazed, the farmer smiled and said, "Maybe."

The next day the farmer's son decided to attempt to tame one of the new wild horses. He set up the saddle and climbed on top to ride it. In a panic, the wild horse leaped up on its hind legs and threw the farmer's son off to the floor. He suffered a broken leg from the fall.

All the neighbors came around that evening and said that it was too bad and it was just an unlucky turn of events.

Unfazed, the farmer smiled and said, "Maybe."

The next week the army recruitment office came by to the village looking for people to enroll into the military. When they came to the farmer's son, they rejected him because of his broken leg.

All the neighbors came around and said, "That's so great," and, "He's so lucky."

Unfazed, the farmer smiled and said, "Maybe."[76]

The course of nature is infinitely complex; we never know everything that's in store for us. The story of the wise farmer shows that we don't have enough foresight to know whether an occurrence is ultimately of a positive or a negative nature. Like a fish that has spent its entire life swimming, we may have an idea that we're going through something, but we don't know exactly what it is. All we know is our present experience, and that's all we need to know for now. In the future we might be able to know more, but like Steve Jobs said, we can't connect the dots looking forward.

We should attempt to approach each situation in life with an understanding that an experience isn't "good" or "bad" in nature; it just *is*. Our focus should be with where our body is, on fully involving ourselves in what's happening in the current moment. This perspective eventually reveals that life happens *for* us, not *to* us. And it's the perspective that puts us in positions of self-empowerment, strengthening our resolve to bring about an opportunity or benefit. With such self-assurance, the so-called unbearableness of uncomfortable situations becomes nothing but a challenge—potential for growth.

Our task is to rise above our emotions, or better yet, duck below them, reminding ourselves that problems are inevitable. By assuming complete responsibility, we hold ourselves accountable to learning about and finding solutions to our unfavorable circumstances. The sooner we understand and accept that the mind is just like any other muscle, the sooner we can begin to effectively strengthen it. We are simply problem solvers presented with puzzles, and that's all there is to it.

The alternative is to view problems we face as unfair or unbeatable and deny our own ability to improve. This way of viewing our circumstances only magnifies our troubles, making it difficult to even show up to make an attempt. When we view life as unfair, we turn our incredible mental faculties against us; we're more likely to be irrational and to mismanage our imagination, perception, and willpower. Like this, it's increasingly difficult to extract lessons or knowledge from any sort of experience. And if the mind can't assign any significant meaning to the situation it's faced with, it grips onto it with regret.

The only good that can come from regret is its usefulness in helping us learn from our mistakes, but too much regret isn't beneficial. When we cling to our past mistakes—when we look back and see nothing but unresolved faults—our guilt lingers, and we develop self-hatred or shame. There is a way through though, and it involves letting go.

There are no *mistakes*, just *occurrences*. Every situation, no matter how uncomfortable, is shaping, chiseling, molding, and preparing us for what's to come. By surrendering personal desires, preferences, judgments, and fixed ideas, we foster natural growth and find harmony with the way things are—we learn to adapt and live pleasantly and effectively in an imperfect world with imperfect beings.

"Only to the extent that we expose ourselves over and over to annihilation can that which is indestructible in us be found." —*Pema Chodron*

"Anything standing
tall without balance is
guaranteed to fall.

14 MAINTAINING BALANCE

There was once a pair of acrobats—a teacher and a student. The teacher was a poor widower and the student was a young girl by the name of Meda. These acrobats performed each day on the streets in order to earn enough to eat.

Their act consisted of the teacher balancing a tall bamboo pole on his head while the little girl climbed slowly to the top. Once on the top, she remained there while the teacher walked along the ground.

Both performers had to maintain complete focus and balance in order to prevent any injury from occurring and to complete the performance. One day, the teacher said to the pupil:

"Listen, Meda, I will watch you and you watch me, so that we can help each other maintain concentration and balance and prevent an accident. Then we'll surely earn enough to eat."

But the little girl was wise. She answered, "Dear master, I think it would be better for each of us to watch ourself. To look after oneself means to look after both of us. That way I am sure we will avoid any accidents and earn enough to eat."[77]

The Importance of Balance

When we speak of intelligence, we often only think of the cognitive faculties of the mind: memory and reason. However, the heart and gut are also incredibly powerful information processing centers, with neurons of their own. In a way, we have three brains: the thinking brain, the emotional brain, and the instinctual brain. Each one of these centers can sense, feel, learn, and remember. All human experience is created through these three centers of intelligence, and the best human experiences are created when these centers are healthy and balanced.

Most people are familiar with the thinking powers of the brain, but few are aware of the incredible capabilities of the gut and heart. For example, not many people know that the gut produces about ninety-five percent of the body's serotonin (the feel-good chemical that regulates our mood).[78] Also, the gut houses about seventy percent of the body's immune system.[79] These brief pieces of information show how sadness, low energy, and foggy thinking can be linked directly to the digestive system and the foods we eat. This is important because our emotional states and energy levels have a direct impact on our thinking and overall level of performance.

The heart plays a critical role with how we show up also. Scientists have confirmed that the heart's fields are continuously interacting with every cell both within and around the body. The electrical field the heart produces is about sixty times greater in amplitude than the brain, and the magnetic field it produces is over one hundred times greater in strength.[80] Our hearts are in a constant state of neurological, biochemical, biophysical, and energetic communication with our entire biological systems and even with the systems in our surrounding environments. So, information about an individual's emotional state is encoded in the heart's magnetic field and transmitted throughout the body and into the external world. When we're out of balance, it doesn't just affect us, but everything around us too—friends, family, pets, customers, employees, etc. Our hearts' have incredible qualities to influence through emotion. And with what scientists have labeled "heart-brain communication"—a synchronization between the "feeling brain" and "thinking brain"—we can access incredible depths of intelligence within us.[81]

Through the mind, we recognize logic, reason, and imagination; through the heart, we identify feelings; and through the gut, instincts. With all three cultivated and synchronized together, we naturally tap into much deeper realms of our intuition. The sensitivity to the happenings in life opens us up to a state of mind where we have the hunches and spontaneous inspirations to make decisions that have profound impacts on our quality of life.

Anything standing tall without balance is guaranteed to fall. If we plan to grow as an expression of life, sooner or later, we'll discover that this human organism has a natural balance to maintain. The requirements for that balance are self-awareness and a method for centering ourselves (which we will discuss later in this chapter). Because inner stability allows us to approach circumstances with composure and intelligence, having our own balance as a priority is simply the sensible thing to do.

As Lao Tzu described, "At the center of your being you have the answer; you know who you are, and you know what you want."

I have many memories of my childhood, but one that's distinct is an evening when I was in the car with my father. As we drove down the four-laned-highway in Los Angeles, he pointed out that if we were to stay in one of the middle lanes, we would have possible openings on both the left and the right side in case we suddenly needed to move out of our lane. About a couple decades later, I was reminded of my father's words when I came across Alan Watts' advice, "Stay in the center, and you will be ready to move in any direction."

The Buddhists speak of the "middle way," a path that avoids all extremes.[82] The middle way is the place between poverty and an excessive desire for more. The place between abstinence and indulgence. The place between reflection and implementation. People on the path of the middle way understand the needs of the stomach versus the desires of the tongue. They eat candy, but the candy isn't part of their diet. If they want to enjoy cake, they take just one or two bites and they are satisfied. The middle way maintains harmony and peace within our minds—it's the path of moderation. People in the middle way are kind, but they don't allow others to take advantage of them. They trust but aren't deceived. They are content but never stop improving.

Thus, inclinations to turn to any extremes signal some discontentment with life and a mismanagement of our intellect—something is bound to be out of balance in one or more areas of life.

The Four Branches

Like how a vehicle uses four tires to travel down the road, people seeking balanced lives must continually sustain and advance each of the four major branches of life: personal, professional, family, and social. Our personal lives include our relationships with ourselves; with our physical bodies; with our intellectual, emotional, and spiritual wellbeing; with our hobbies, pleasures, and entertainment—basically, the things we do in our private time. Our professional lives include our careers, our accomplishments, our finances, and anything else related to our contributions to our professions. Then we have our family lives and social lives, which involve the time we spend cultivating relationships with those closest and dearest to us and the time we spend cultivating our relationships with the rest of the world.

Much like the tires on the car, all the four branches of life are interconnected. If one tire is deflated, it affects the safety of the entire vehicle. If we're lacking in one part of our lives, the disharmony will eventually seep into the other parts. You know how true this statement is if you've ever argued with loved ones because of financial obligations you're unable to meet, or if you've ever experienced a heartbreak and consequently couldn't fulfill your duties effectively at work. To combat this disharmony, we must expand our perspectives and find balance at the root of all the branches—the self.

Since one decision in some aspect of life impacts decisions made in other aspects of life, we can credit any sense of success to the choices we make. Interestingly, it's not so important to continually make the *right* choices; it's more important to continually make choices that are aligned with our *intentions*. The less significance we place on making right choices, the more momentum we create to keep us moving. Right choices inevitably come about as a result of experience, and experience is often gained through making the wrong choices.

Several years ago, I met two individuals both in the early stages of building their own businesses. The first individual, whom I'll call Tod, was always working on something. I don't remember a time when he didn't have something new that he was doing. The second individual, Ron, would work on something, then find himself stuck between options. You can say he was a more calculating fellow, looking for a sure win—perfection; however, this didn't work to his advantage. After some time, I found out Tod's business had taken off. After visiting him one day, I noticed a bunch of unused flyers, unpromoted products, idle business cards, and many other promotional materials in his office. When I asked him why they were just sitting there, he told me he couldn't use them because they all had mistakes or outdated information printed on them. When I inquired further, he told me it wasn't just the promotional material; about eighty percent of the work he'd done in the last several months was just to keep the momentum going and the inspiration flowing— only about twenty percent of the work he'd done actually made a difference in moving his business forward. I realized that while Ron was deciding on which color background to have on his business card, Tod was already introducing himself to potential clients. Even though Tod made several mistakes and spent a lot of his time on things that didn't matter much in the short term, he kept making progress by continuously making decisions and acting upon them. Not only did he feel better as a result, but he also built a successful company in the process. Ron, on the other hand, eventually gave up on his dream of owning a business.

The principle here is much like that of riding a bicycle: it's difficult to balance while the bike is standing still, but when the rider and bike are in motion, it's much easier to stay on the bike. All that's

left then is the direction we go, and for that, we can look to what we prioritize in our lives—where our attention mostly goes.

The Need for Prioritizing

Prioritizing not only gives us direction but also helps us recognize the sacrifices we must make. When we don't identify the things that matter to us, it's easy to become distracted (the term for entrepreneurs in business is *shiny object syndrome*). The fear of missing out on *the next happening* disrupts focus and causes attention to drift from where it's needed—what's truly important. Saying "no" and setting boundaries for ourselves can be difficult for some. However, when we have our priorities clearly defined, it becomes easier to make the necessary sacrifices—usually trading immediate gratification for a bigger reward later.

Every business owner that held a job prior to working completely for themselves made a decision to leave their job because of prioritizing. The time we have is limited and so is the energy we have that we can invest. When our attention is placed in one area, it can't be anywhere else. Likewise, there's a cost associated with every decision that we make; that cost is any benefit that could have been gained from any other decision made. In other words, when we decide against something, we decide against just that thing. However, when we decide for something, we're simultaneously deciding against every other thing in the realm of what we decided for. For example, when we decide to engage in a monogamous relationship with someone, we're saying no to every other potential partner—the opportunity cost is anyone else that we could be in a relationship with. The full-time entrepreneur, realizing that the steady paycheck and reliable position stood in the way of their desire to build and grow something of their own, eventually dropped the job and invested more of their time and efforts in their own business. When we understand our opportunity costs, instead of saying "no" to sacrifice, we can reframe our point of view and say "yes" to desired outcomes—to balance, to growth, and ultimately, to happiness.

We have only twenty-four hours in a day and seven days in a week. If we want to spend that precious time wisely, we need to know what's important to us. To be productive is to know our priorities and to unapologetically reserve the right to say "no" to things not aligned with them. For example, if financial independence is our priority, a regular job and eight-hour workday may not be enough. In such case, we'll need to find other means of delivering value in the marketplace. We'll likely need to sacrifice some of the remaining sixteen hours, trading our time on social media, television, video games, and sleep for time to learn from books, mentors, and online resources—anything that will improve our case.

Sometimes, even if we know what we should do, we don't feel like doing it. This feeling itself is a sign of some inner imbalance. It's a call to center ourselves.

The Ways to Find Balance

If we're not centered, we're not fully present and capable of being effective on any significant level; so, anything we do—exercising, conducting a business meeting, conversing with a loved one—is half done. One might fill their schedule and feel busy as can be, yet still be completely unproductive. Busyness doesn't necessarily equal progress, and people who are *too busy* rarely make meaningful progress. The centered person, on the other hand, can make time for themselves. Consequently, they can make time for the things that matter—their priorities.

Centering one's self means simply creating peace within, in order to be completely present with what's without. Using certain exercises, visualizations, and meditations, we can produce a coherent state, and through the intelligence of our body, ease ourselves back into the present moment.

A simple yet effective method of meditation to achieve this inner sense of peace is to sit quietly, close your eyes, and focus your attention at the center of your chest or the area of your heart. Using your diaphragm, breathe deeply and more slowly than usual into your belly, but use your imagination to visualize your breath flowing in and out of your chest area or heart. Once you have a stable rhythm that feels natural (the length of your inhale naturally matches the length of your exhale), focus your efforts into activating a feeling of gratitude. You can do this by thinking about someone or something you care about, things that are going well for you, or a place you enjoy. If you're having trouble generating a feeling of gratitude, just focus on a feeling of calmness. Continue breathing this feeling into your heart or the center of your chest until you feel peace on the inside. Things should feel like they've slowed down and balanced internally.

You can use this meditation method several times a day, practically anywhere, and feel results in as little as five to ten minutes. It will help you immediately reduce stress and feel positive, aligned, focused, and energized. Creating a habit of this practice will help you access deeper states of creativity and intuition, and that will significantly improve your decision-making abilities.

We're all born to die, but more importantly, we're born to live. We live life in each moment, and the more present we are in those moments, the more effective we'll be. When we apply daily methods of centering ourselves, we cultivate true balance. And when we have true balance, we make choices that bring about true progress.

"From ancient cultures to today, like a thread through the needle of time, the heart appears as a symbol and source of health, wisdom, and intuition." —Dr. Joe Dispenza

Our "enemies" are
the shadows we
ourselves cast.

15 INTERCONNECTING HUMANS

The story of the two travelers and the wise farmer:

A traveler came upon a wise old farmer working his field beside the road.

Ready to take a break from his journey, the wanderer hailed the countryman, who seemed happy enough to take a break himself and talk for a moment.

"What type of people live in the next town?" asked the stranger.

"What were the people like where you've come from?" replied the farmer, answering the question with another question.

"They were bad. Troublemakers, and lazy too. The most selfish people in the world, and not one of them is to be trusted. I'm happy to be leaving the crooks; and I never want to return."

"Is that so?" replied the old farmer. "Well, I'm afraid that you'll find the same type in the next town."

Disappointed, the traveler dragged himself on his way, and the farmer returned to his work.

Sometime later, another stranger, coming from the same direction, hailed the farmer.

"What sort of people live in the next town?" he asked.

"What were the people like where you've come from?" replied the farmer once again.

"They were some of the best people in the world. Hardworking, honest, and friendly. I'm sorry to be leaving them, but I must continue on in my journey."

"Fear not," said the farmer. "You'll find the same sort in the next town."[83]

Appreciating Relationships

Because we experience life through our senses, the foundation of reality itself is a relationship. Light is born from a relationship between energy and eyes. Scents from a relationship between energy and the nose. Sounds from a relationship between energy and ears. Texture from a relationship between energy and skin. And taste from a relationship between energy and the tongue.

Thanks to our senses in combination with our mental faculties, we ourselves conjure the world, and we conjure it in accordance with what type of organism we are. The reality experienced by the fly is completely different than reality experienced by the spider. As said by Charles Addams, "Normal is an illusion. What is normal for the spider is chaos for the fly." But even between humans there are differences between what the experience of reality is like. Because we each have our own unique biological and neurological make-up, one person conjures one type of world, and another person conjures another type of world. Between all the different individuals, no two experiences of life are exactly the same.

Although it might be easy to inspect a person's life from the outside, to judge his or her experience, we never really know what reality from their perspective is like. Someone could have incredible wealth, a large network of successful friends, and a seemingly healthy lifestyle, but their minds could be filled with turmoil and their hearts with loneliness. Another could have only enough for the day yet be completely content and joyful. That's why it's best to never judge another's life, but to focus on our own circumstances instead.

The easiest way to measure the quality of our own lives is through our relationships—with ourselves, our families, our friends; with work and business acquaintances, strangers, and even those who wish badly for us. Because our experiences with others are reflections of what's inside ourselves, each association can reveal insights into the depths of our own beings—our deepest beliefs and ways of viewing ourselves and the world around us.

So what are the stories we're telling ourselves?

We each have a story for every individual that we cross paths with. Some stories are more profound than others, but each contributes to our worldviews. On some level, they either help empower us or leave us feeling inadequate and exhausted. Remember the story of the two wolves fighting? (See chapter twelve.) Our internal stories are feeding either the wolf of positive nature or the wolf of negative nature.

In previous chapters, we've touched on the importance of our relationships with ourselves, with our self-images, and with our higher Self. We've reviewed how our beliefs affect our behavior and the decisions we make and how our perspectives relate to our emotional responses, completely directing our life experiences. Now that we understand that our relationships with ourselves are the starting points from which we approach the world and other relationships, we can take a closer look into this idea of the relationship with self.

Being Alone vs. Feeling Alone

Many people feel lonely even when surrounded by others. Particularly in large cities, where the majority of humans live, people report feeling just as lonely as if they lived in solitude.[84] Thus, we can conclude that loneliness is a creation of our own mentality. Since we have ourselves to live with for the rest of our lives, this can be a huge problem.

We can investigate the psychology of how loneliness sprouts in the minds of these individuals. When we inquire into the perspectives of these people, we find that not only do they often not know how to connect with others, often they're holding subconscious self-centeredness, focusing only on their own needs and desires.[85] Their mindset is rooted in "I lack." This self-centered perspective, which we're all susceptible to, feeds fear and creates discontentment within ourselves, thus revealing the loneliness.

Being alone and feeling alone are vastly different states. Many people spend most of their days in solitude but never feel lonely.[86] These individuals, along with those who are very sociable, share common views about human life, and they approach life, including themselves, with sincerity and openness. Because they're open and accepting, these people can't help but naturally look for the good in others. This causes them to feel connected with and empathetic toward others. As a result, they have fewer unpleasant interactions with others, and with themselves when they're alone.

This attitude results from compassion toward others and toward ourselves, and it counters fear and apprehension. There is no desire to act in certain ways or say certain things to be liked and accepted. Instead, there's openness and honest, sincere expression, and these qualities in turn create opportunities to receive positive responses and to have meaningful exchanges. When this positive perspective about ourselves and our fellow human beings is missing from our lives, even those closest to us can make us feel closed off, cold, and uncomfortable.

The history of Joseph Stalin, a leader of the Soviet Union, provides a clear example of what can happen when our perspectives are not aligned with those of our fellow human beings. The more Stalin accomplished and the more he grew in power, the more ruthless and cruel he became. His lack of compassion, which created an absence of inner peace, led to insecurity and fear—to the point where he was suspicious of even his most trusted generals and companions, later executing them without mercy. Believing that humans were incapable of genuine warmheartedness, he saw everyone as his enemies, and he often thought that those closest to him were conspiring against him. The cruel and ruthless perspectives Stalin held led to his paranoia and violent actions.[87]

Even with success, fame, power, and interpersonal relationships, if we don't have peace of mind, we can't feel genuinely connected with others or our environment. Instead, we'll create mental attitudes that manifest feelings of loneliness. Science proves that a negative state of mind leads to negative mental and physical health; therefore, without internal peace, we can't enjoy life with good health for long.

Being Connected

With enough observation, we'll realize how our thoughts and emotions spread and affect those around us and even our communities and society. Modern science, particularly quantum mechanics through the notion of quantum entanglement, is just now uncovering what Buddhist teachings expressed long ago. Namely, the principle of connectedness, which states that all things are linked on the deepest levels.

Since loneliness comes as a result of our perspectives, we can counter loneliness by adjusting how we view our relationships with other people. When we desire peace for others, connect with them, and help them, we nurture our own inner peace. The deeper we understand other humans' emotions and sufferings, the more we can cultivate empathy and connect with others—if you knew an individual's whole story, you'd be less inclined to judge them for the way they are.

However, without awareness of the kinds of connectedness we're seeking, we can obstruct our abilities to form strong relationships. It's possible for us to turn toward a darker perspective of connectedness consisting of desire for control and manipulation. This happens when we're so emotionally attached to an individual that we cannot let them be themselves. We need them to be a specific way, based on our own self-centered needs. We try to shape and mold them how we see fit, oblivious or apathetic to their own personal needs. Like

Alan Watts comically expressed, "'Kindly let me help you or you will drown,' said the monkey, putting the fish safely up a tree."

If our idea of connectedness leads us to believe that we are knotted with others, we're approaching life with a sense of insecurity. We can sometimes be compassionate and empathetic only to the extent that others are compassionate and empathetic with us. When this happens, we convince ourselves that we're no longer lonely and that we finally have someone to face life's problems with. This isn't what's actually happening though. This type of self-centered longing for another person creates unhealthy dependence. The communication and behavior come from fear, not from openness. Our entire feeling of self-worth becomes contingent on others' acceptance. And as soon as no one is around to keep us distracted and comfortable, the loneliness bursts back in.

This approach to building relationships is like turning a wheel down only so the other side can go up. Those of us who struggle with these kinds of relationships are firmly, and likely unknowingly, attached to the idea of doing something only for a reward. Approaching others in this way isn't going to cure loneliness. All it does is create the illusion of security. As a result, we become needy and insecure, since our relationships come from a foundation of fraud.

True connectedness isn't based on a contract of "be this way or do this for me and I'll be that way or do that for you." Rather, it's based on the belief that love without reward is valuable. True connectedness is based in the fact that all human beings—not just the ones who are precious to us—have a natural right to happiness and peace of mind.

Strong interpersonal connections are crucial to our existence. Research shows that people who have close ties with others whom they can turn to for support and encouragement are more likely to not only survive but to thrive in times of difficulty. And this type of security can be created through something as simple as engaging others with openness and with the understanding that we are all experiencing life together.

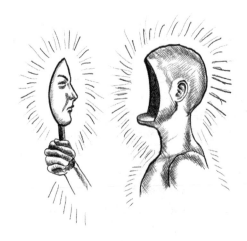

This mindset of interconnectedness becomes especially important when we have to deal with those who wish badly for us or purposely harm us. Often such actions cause us to carry feelings of anger or hatred, and sometimes we may be tempted to strike back. To counteract these harmful emotions, we must use reason and understanding to direct our thoughts toward more productive ends, looking for new points of view. Once we realize that no person is all bad and that we're all human beings just trying our best to survive, be accepted, and be happy, then we can develop compassion and empathy even for our enemies. These sentiments will in turn foster growth and happiness. We may even come to realize that the bad we see in others is a projection of our own shortcomings; and maybe we'll understand that our "enemies" are the shadows we ourselves cast.

Carl Jung said, "Everything that irritates us about others can lead us to an understanding of ourselves." When we see behaviors we don't like, the question we should ask ourselves is, "Where have I behaved like this in my own life?" or, "Under what conditions might I myself behave like this?" Answering these questions won't only make us more accepting of others, but it can also take us to new heights of perception and can raise our self-awareness.

To understand our emotions better, we can put aside our own perspectives and jump into the shoes of other individuals. Using our imagination, we can form an idea of how other people see situations. There's always another side to every story. If we can suspend our judgements to see situations from other angles, we can understand other people's feelings and viewpoints and show them respect. This empathy will help us in all our interpersonal relations.

As with any practice, we must repeatedly reinforce these ideas of interconnectedness and empathy to create lasting change. Our previous habits will want to counteract these new approaches to relationships. With patience and tolerance, though, we can change. By increasing our compassion and empathy, we can learn to view negative emotions as opportunities for growth and progress. With this perspective, we can actually view our enemies as our greatest allies in personal development. Who but those who incite friction within us can give us opportunities to practice patience and acceptance? Without even knowing it, they help us grow mentally and emotionally strong. Imagine their confusion when we tell them "thank you" someday.

When we focus on this outlook and on the fact that other human beings are just doing their best to survive and find inner peace, it's much easier to find better ways of dealing with difficult individuals.

If we truly wish to deepen connections, we must be open to new ways of seeing people. If we continue to view others through the same lenses we're used to, we'll develop a rigid view and it will limit our ability to notice any positive changes in them or in ourselves. Further, we'll miss chances to provide helpful encouragement toward the positive changes we'd like to see.

Without connectedness, compassion, and empathy toward one another, we rely on our influence over others to provide a way out of the loneliness. Isn't it more rewarding to approach relationships from a place of affection based on the commonalities we share? If we stop to think about it, there truly are so many commonalities. And when we make the effort to look for those commonalities and create affection, eventually our loneliness dissipates, and the harmful effects of anger and hatred weaken.

Ultimately, growth in relationships is a sign of growth in life. Whether it's with ourselves, our life partners, friends, customers, business acquaintances, or even strangers, we cannot overlook the importance of healthy relations. We are all interconnected with one another in more ways than we're consciously aware of. This understanding leads to an abundant and satisfying life full of the deep, meaningful relationships we all seek.

"If you know who you are, and I know who I am, how many of us are there?" —Unknown

Today's education in society separates daily life into work and play, making us look at work as something that we must do because we need money.

16 DEMYSTIFYING MONEY

Healthy Groceries—$100—"No, that's too expensive."
Night Out Bar Hopping—$100—"That's reasonable. Much-needed fun!"

Membership to a Fitness Club—$150—"That's absurd. I can't afford that right now!"
New Gaming Equipment—$150—"Oh, that's a great deal!"

Self-Improvement Course—$1,000—"That's way too expensive."
New Computer—$1,000—"Yes. It's a necessity, and I'll use it every day."

The Education of Today

Modern society seems to be infatuated with money and the accumulation of it. Especially for the entrepreneur, money plays a big role in life. Unfortunately, not many seem to understand its true function or its position in their life. To really demystify and understand money, we must first look at how we're educated to view ourselves, our lives, and our purposes for living. Understanding these will give us an idea of what's influencing our decision-making, particularly in the area of our drive to accumulate more money. Then we can better understand the role that money plays in our lives, what we can do with it, and how we should engage with it.

The systems of education we have in place are expected to teach us how to create quality lifestyles and earn money. People believe that if they've gone to school, studied, and earned high grades, they'll be prepared to navigate life in healthy, happy, and fulfilling ways. They believe that if they have received training and earned a degree in a specialized field, they'll have the skills necessary to earn enormous amounts of money and live completely secure, free, and fulfilled lives. Unfortunately, most of today's public educational systems do not satisfy these objectives. Albert Einstein commented on this with his observation, "Education is what remains after one has forgotten what one has learned in school."

If the most important lessons of life—such as the true nature of our beings, awareness over ourselves, and the mechanics of how our bodies and minds work—aren't in the curriculum, how can we expect to confidently navigate life? The curricula give information and knowledge about the different roles we can play in life but not about how to think for ourselves; instead, they teach us to memorize and adopt the thoughts of others. The aftermath is a society filled with materialistic viewpoints, people who know how to work and manage their gadgets and schedules better than their own minds and bodies, and people who busy themselves with *things* instead of being completely present with *people*. In short, many modern education systems create people who love things and use people. This underlying impression distorts our understanding about our lives' purposes.

The Truth About the Future

Philo (20 BC–50 AD) said, "Today means boundless and inexhaustible eternity. Months and years and all periods of time are concepts of men, who gauge everything by number; but the true name of eternity is Today."

In a system that trains us to have rigid views and attachments to others' ideas that we've adopted as our own, it's easy to go through life with the biggest misconception: the idea of the future.

Our idea of the future causes us to always be preparing for something as we age. It alters our interpretations of the purpose of life into being a results-based game of survival with an emphasis on accumulation. Because our education systems overtrain our rational minds and undertrain our intuitive minds, our imagination can sometimes work against us, putting us in a restless state of anxiety about what might happen—about not being properly prepared.

This future-thinking mentality is mostly a result of our ability to think about our own lives; our innate gift of metacognition is turned against us. Because we know that our lives are temporary and that we're all mortal, society conditions us to always try to prepare for when we're closer to death. That's how our culture developed the idea of retirement, that moment in life when we have the wealth and leisure to do all the things we've always wanted to do. It's when we've paid our dues and can begin to truly enjoy the freedoms of life.

It's a joke—and a bad one at that.

After following society's guidelines, coloring inside the lines, and doing what we're told, very few of us actually get to experience that luxurious type of retirement; and if we do, by that time many of us are too weak to experience much pleasure from it. What's more likely is that we're living in regret for having gone through our life sacrificing the things we wanted to do for meaningless pursuits in trying to create a sense of security for our "future."

The future is just a thought—a word, a label. Tomorrow never comes. Eternity is always in the present moment. We're only alive right now; everything else is a distraction from what *is*. Thus, we must always be completely engaged in what we're doing in the present moment—that's the only way we can be genuinely living life fully. And there's nothing more meaningful or more real than facing the tough facts of the immediate present.

Alan Watts said,

> Unless one is able to live fully in the present, the future is a hoax. There is no point whatever in making plans for a future which you will never be able to enjoy. When your plans mature, you will still be living for some other future beyond. You will never, never be able to sit back

with full contentment and say, 'Now, I've arrived!' Your entire education has deprived you of this capacity because it was preparing you for the future, instead of showing you how to be alive now.[88]

When we don't apply this understanding of the "future" in our lives, we go on contributing to current backward systems and viewpoints. Although having direction and plans for a future could benefit us, we must experience our lives fully emerged in the present moment. The alternative is to turn life into a game of accumulation and preparation for an idea in our imagination that never arrives.

The Truth About Money

Today's education in society separates daily life into work and play, making us look at work as something that we must do because we need money. Really, such a mindset compels us to have jobs so boring that no one else will take them, just so we can get paid more to do them. Then the purpose of making the money is to go home and enjoy that money. We plan to enjoy the second half of the day as play; but for the average person who lives for the future, that

doesn't really happen. More realistically, we go home tired, drained, or exhausted and eat uninteresting and unhealthy dinners, then we watch electronic reproductions of life through plastic boxes with glass screens. The *play* part of our lives gets pushed into the future again, to the weekend.

"You need to give up five precious days of the week because money is important" is a lie; further, it's a robbery of life. When we believe that money is the important thing, we waste all our time. We do things we don't like doing just so we can get money to go on living. In other words, we do things we don't like just so we can go on doing things we don't like.

This idea is so discreetly ingrained in modern culture that it even drives some of us to trade our most precious possessions—our time, attention, health, friends, family, and even our integrity—for some cash. A recent poll uncovered that a staggering 85% of people are unhappy with their jobs. We're exchanging our real riches for temporary affluence and calling it an even trade.[89] As the brilliant social psychologist, Erich Fromm, pointed out, "Modern man is alienated from himself, from his fellow men, and from nature. His main aim is profitable exchange of his skills, knowledge, and of himself."

Much like *sex, religion*, and *politics*, the word *money* can ignite powerful feelings. It makes some people feel guilty when they have it, and it makes others feel ashamed when they don't. It stirs up feelings of desire and even excitement. Some say money is the root of all evil, and others say it's the key to happiness. Whatever thoughts or emotions we may hold toward money, we have to agree that, at its root, money is simply a means of exchange. It's as good as a pebble, just as long as somebody wants that pebble.

Just as a clock is used to measure time, money is used to measure wealth. The clock is not time itself, just as money is not wealth itself. The way people earn their money (through wages, or in the case of business owners, profits) is by trading something else of value for it. Thus, money is produced through an exchange of value. Whether it be through time and skills or through a product or service, value is transferred from one end to the other. The increase and decrease of a person's finances are just a consequence of this transition.

Unfortunately, there's no running from it: money is a part of the system we live in, a system in which every object's price is determined by the amount of life people are willing to give up for it. We must accept the fact that we all need money; and really, it's only because we've all agreed that we need money. In our imaginations, money has become the metaphorical scale that measures the value of exchange between people.

Money is a tool. It has the power to create and the power to destroy. It can be useful, helping turn dreams into reality; and it can be fearsome, causing regret and anxiety. While it can bring comfort and luxury, it also feeds insecurities, jealousy, and hatred. Today, with our technological advancements, money can add convenience to our lifestyles; but at the same time it can be a burden that we're continually chasing, keeping us from actually enjoying those lifestyles. Money can take us to places we've never been, and it can keep us away from the places we want to be. It can take care of problems for the people we love; it can keep us away from the people who need us most. Even if we have the most remarkable financial gains, if we don't master money, it will master us.

The Need to Understand Money

Our culture has been filled with many myths that revolve around financial education. Many of us grow up with self-sabotaging beliefs about money. Because so many of us are uninformed, we often take ignorant risks. Ultimately, the myths about money have conditioned many false perspectives about wealth. Like a tail that tries to wag the dog, we try to get more money, pursuing wealth.

With the way the world is today, financial education is actually one of the most powerful types of education available. It helps us understand that while the attachment to money may be the root of all evil, money itself is not. Financial education helps us understand that money is an illusion: a series of numbers on a computer screen at the bank, rarely even backed by gold anymore. Money can undoubtedly allow us to create extraordinary lifestyles, but it *does not* and *must not* determine our sense of security, our freedom, or our feelings of empowerment. Moreover, it shouldn't govern our ability to feel alive or our sense of self-worth. Thankfully, once financial education helps us put money in its proper place, we can learn how to win the financial game.

Financial education also reminds us to be appreciative of what money can bring us. Often it seems like we as a culture are more focused on the dollar bill than on what we purchase. Rather than appreciating the experiences we pay for, we're too occupied being distressed about their financial costs. Instead of expressing gratitude for the roofs over our heads, we get upset when it's time to exchange the numbers we've collected in our bank accounts for the shelter and security we have—as if the digital numbers were more valuable than a warm, dry, peaceful living space. By neglecting our real riches like this, we cultivate a worldview of lack and limitation. That's when all our problems seem to become money problems. It's the birth of a poverty mindset: a belief system that life is full of scarcity, that there isn't enough for everyone, that money is difficult to earn, and that it's hard to get what you want.

It should be clear by now that our perspectives of certain things govern our experiences with them. This being the case, we can change our experiences with something—like money—when we change the way we look at it. By applying this concept to our finances, we realize that appreciating our money can change our experience with it too. Even if this perspective doesn't stop us from wanting more, at the very least it can help us be more grateful for what we do have.

Having a good perspective on money is important because as our income increases, so does the significance of the role money plays in our lives and the power of our spending habits. We must realize that money doesn't change us; it just makes us more of what we already are. If we spend money on nonessentials and overpay for luxuries and conveniences, we'll continue to do so on a much larger level when we come across more money. The problem is never money, but values and principles.

Understanding that money isn't a cure-all helps us move further in quality of life. Take the cashier at a supermarket, for example, looking to move up in the workplace. The cashier shouldn't just fulfill regular cashier responsibilities if he or she expects to one day become a manager of the store. Instead, the cashier must take on a larger viewpoint. The cashier must enthusiastically contribute to the success and progress of the business. Only then can the cashier's knowledge of the store really matter—when the heart is aligned with the actions.

Another example is a bee gathering honey for the queen. The bee never stops to think about the flower, honey, or queen bee. It just goes on doing what it does for the sake of doing what it does. There's no emphasis on the results or rewards in the future, just on the quality of what's being done now.

The cashier (the earnest seeker of self-sufficiency) needs to find a way to work just like the bee—for something deeper than the honey, for something deeper than the money, for something deeper than themselves.

There are two major attitudes in workplaces today. The best way to describe the first attitude is *forfeiture*—clock in and clock out, all for the love of that great illusion: security through money. The second attitude, though, is held by employees who are at peace with their work. They work with an actual desire to do what they're doing, and they gain a feeling of significance from what they do. They achieve a true sense of fulfillment because they lose themselves in their efforts. As they work wholeheartedly, the work becomes play— they're completely present and there's no separation between now and the future, between what's being given and what's to be received.

A Brazilian jujitsu professor of mine, who has been an accomplished practitioner for over thirty years, once told me it's his perspective that allows him to perform and communicate the techniques the way he does. The years of hard work we put into mastering anything are also years put into developing proper perspectives.

When we're masters at anything, we see the processes differently than others do; we can view the bigger picture and separate it from the immediate nuances. Our belief systems adjust. We become more aware, we behave differently, and we allow our natural intelligence to perform accordingly. These results of fine-tuning our viewpoints to put things in their proper context enable us to navigate difficult tasks and circumstances better.

This principle of refining our outlooks is no different when it comes to life strategy, finance, and career decisions. Learning to become aware of others' ideas we've adopted as our own—which eventually influence our decision-making—gives us more control and security in life than any amount of money could.

"When everything is subject to money, then the scarcity of money makes everything scarce, including the basis of human life and happiness. Such is the life of the slave—one whose actions are compelled by threat to survival. Perhaps the deepest indication of our slavery is the monetization of time." —Charles Eisenstein[90]

When we decide on
the roles we want
to play, we're at the
same time choosing
the value we're going
to deliver and the
impacts we're going
to make.

17 SEEING THROUGH THE ENTREPRENEUR'S LENS

Once upon a time there was a businessman passing by a small city town in Armenia.

As he traveled down a busy street, he noticed a man selling pastries from a small vending cart.

He was drawn in by the big smile the man had on his face and the smell of fresh pastries made from apricots.

Experiencing a warm, friendly welcome, he decided to try one.

After just the first bite, he was overwhelmed by the pleasant taste and asked the pastry salesman, "What's your process to make these pastries?"

The pastry salesman replied, "Oh, I just pick some apricots with my two young children. My wife does the baking. It doesn't take her long, and she enjoys it."

"In that case, why don't you pick more and have her bake in bigger batches? I see you're almost sold out, and it's not even mid-day yet." The businessman was curious.

"We don't need much. What I make from these small trips is enough for us," replied the pastry salesman.

The businessman became interested, "So, what do you do when you've sold your supply?"

The pastry salesman replied pleasantly, "Well, I usually go shopping with my family to purchase materials for the next morning's batch—my children and I go out into the fields early in the morning to pick fresh apricots for her. Afterwards, when I've sold the supply and she's done baking, we play with the kids together. Then our neighbors and friends come over and we eat, drink, and dance to our favorite music with them."

The businessman, listening attentively, became stunned and began to give the pastry salesman his advice.

"I've started many successful businesses, and all have grown to bring me much wealth. What I'm about to tell you can transform your life and bring you riches you and your family will enjoy. You and your children should pick as many apricots as possible from those fields on each visit, and your wife should bake as many of these fine pastries as she can with them. You will surely sell them all and have enough to buy a bigger cart."

The pastry salesman inquired, "What would I do then?"

A smile grew on the businessman's face, "Then, soon after, once you've saved up enough money, you can purchase a storefront and start your own bakery where you can hire workers to pick the apricots and bake for you. You will become a wealthy businessman like me."

The pastry salesman asked, "What's a simple man like me to do then?"

The businessman replied, "Well, then you and your wife can spend your time doing what you enjoy. You can play with your kids together even be out in the beautiful fields together. You can entertain your guests with good food, drink, and dance to your favorite music with them!"

Confused, the pastry salesperson responded, "Besides the stress of all that work and responsibility, it sounds like my life wouldn't be much different than it is now."

The Entrepreneur Mindset

Now that we've talked about the nature of human beings and the importance of perspective and self-awareness, I want to talk about a critical factor to aligning yourself for self-sufficiency, for success: the entrepreneurial mindset. Modern society seems to idolize entrepreneurship yet has completely neglected the foundation that shapes the craft: entrepreneurial values. When most people think of entrepreneurship, they think in terms of contracts, products, and sales. But behind the physical manifestations of business operations there is a mind that orchestrates all these things.

Just as there are clear and consistent patterns throughout nature (as we discussed in chapter five), there are clear and consistent patterns throughout a successful business organization. The mind behind the scenes organizes these patterns in such a way as to work coherently to produce certain outcomes. For example, the sales department needs to work with the team that's fulfilling the orders; customer service needs to cooperate with the fulfillment team; marketing must cooperate with salespeople. Without the mind behind the scenes and the systems it puts in motion, there would be no harmony between the various departments, no common vision to aspire to.

In this chapter we're going to discuss entrepreneurship applied for business owners. The focus will be more about the mindset and less about the profession; more about perspective *on* businesses and their various functions, and less about operations *in* the business and their procedures. The mindset behind entrepreneurship can be applied to life in general, not just business, because the ideas themselves aid in achieving self-fulfillment as they reinforce interdependence, perseverance, and self-reliance.

By understanding both the micro and the macro, the person applying the entrepreneurial mindset adopts the views and beliefs that enhance his or her ability to spot and create potential opportunities. The person walks into the unknown with nothing but an internal compass and proceeds toward the direction that leads closest to the manifestation of his or her vision. And since the path is filled with adversity, just by showing up to face it the person earns a chance to learn and improve.

The Freedom of Entrepreneurship

The lion that lives in a cage at the zoo is guaranteed shelter, food, security, and medical care for as long as the zoo is around and has a need for the lion. The lion in the wilderness is guaranteed nothing but has complete free will. While most occupational roles in this lifetime allow people to make great livings, many of those roles come with heavy conditions that limit freedom. However, there are some professions that allow individuals almost total independence in lifestyle choice. One of these, if done successfully, is entrepreneurship.

Today, entrepreneurs are viewed as creators; by producing, innovating, and marketing, they change the world around them. In this sense, entrepreneurs can dictate where their lives go almost every day, month, and year. Rather than being accountable for the time they invest—the hours they punch in—they take strict measures to manage their attention, priorities, and values. It's not so much about how many working hours they log but more so how much they get done, how much progress is made. Doing the bare minimum or cutting corners will not fly for entrepreneurs. They work for themselves, and consequently they really do reap what they sow. There's a certain level of integrity involved in that work. If they don't follow through on their commitments or don't own up to their shortcomings, there will be clear and direct repercussions. Entrepreneurs must demonstrate their core values in all their efforts. They must hold themselves accountable and remain open and honest in their communications.

Rather than molding into systems that already exist, entrepreneurs form new systems according to the realities they want to create. Instead of following directions, they generate them, carving out paths for others to follow. Entrepreneurs proactively create life's circumstances, constantly investing in themselves mentally, physically, emotionally, and spiritually.

Like the role of an artist, the role of an entrepreneur is unique to each individual who plays it. Even though the art and products are produced for people to see and experience, artists, as well as entrepreneurs, have their own journeys within themselves to manifest their visions. An incredible amount of self-awareness can be gained while navigating a business in the marketplace. It's a golden opportunity to learn in a short amount of time a great deal about who we are and how we play with others.

The marketplace is like a dojo: it's a mini universe where we test our knowledge and abilities in battles with ourselves—with our egos, our fears, and our behaviors that hold us back from the lives we want. In this arena, practitioners are brought together—not just as opponents in competition but also as partners in cooperation— fully engaged in honest expression, helping each other understand themselves on deeper levels for the genuine growth of all involved. Although desire for sincere advancement is critical here, the goal isn't necessarily to "win." The goal is self-education and self-actualization; it's learning to enjoy the entire process, both wanted and unwanted; it's learning to achieve a higher level of competence to eventually gain mastery. The conflicts we experience in the dojo better prepare us for conflicts in life. We're involved in an endless daily discipline requiring our complete focus and our beginner's mind—the open and eager mind, free from preconceptions.

The Inner Success of Entrepreneurship

Dr. Wayne Dyer once said, "Our beliefs are the invisible ingredients in all our activities." With little observation, we can see how true this statement really is. Here are some common beliefs and thoughts most people will be familiar with:

"I can't do that." "I don't know how." "What if this happens?" "There's so-and-so in the way." "I can't afford it." "I don't have the time." These are all excuses—signs that we're limiting our beliefs. A far more productive approach is to turn these statements into questions: "How can I do that?" "Where can I learn to do that?" "What will I do if this happens?" "How can I persuade so-and-so to help me?" "What can I do to be able to afford this?" "What's most important right now?" These questions open the mind rather than close it.

The reason most individuals don't get what they want is that they haven't really tried. Full of doubt, they do themselves the greatest disservice: they stop themselves from taking on new risks. They stop themselves from failure, and they stop themselves from learning.

Success requires failure. In fact, it demands it. Failure gives us opportunities to learn and to grow. Napoleon Hill, author of *Laws of Success*, expresses this idea clearly in his many books and lectures: "Every adversity, every failure, every heartache carries with it the seed of an equal or greater benefit."[91] Throughout any great undertaking, we must not only be willing to fail but also expect to fail. And when we understand that failure is guaranteed in life, we should choose to fail on the road to what we actually want, to what genuinely matters.

We don't live solely for ourselves. Alone, we would each be just a speck of dust in the wind, a small wave in the massive ocean. In reality, we live for everything and everyone around us. When we decide on the roles we want to play, we're at the same time choosing the value we're going to deliver and the impacts we're going to make. That's where true fulfillment comes from.

With this awareness, successful entrepreneurs are merely vessels for the value that must be delivered to humanity. In other words, they are trusted agents in their communities who can diligently use their knowledge and experience to serve. The wise and mature entrepreneurs, having seen and experienced first-hand the suffering of the world, become instruments to help mankind evolve.

It's been said that when we start to plant trees, knowing that we might never sit in the shade or enjoy the fruits produced, we've begun to understand the meaning of life.

"What are some problems I can help solve thanks to my life experiences?" "What does the world need done that I can lend a hand in doing?" "How can I apply myself in ways that will benefit not only myself but also many others at the same time?"

Questions like these influence the subconscious and activate the reticular activating system differently. (See chapter three for more information about the RAS.) When we adjust our RAS in this way, we see what steps are necessary for our advancement. We allow pieces of the puzzle to come together. Because of neuroplasticity and the conscious will, we can reframe our perspectives and create lasting change both within us and around us. Over time, we guide our minds to work for us instead of against us.

Positioning ourselves for success *with* fulfillment is an inside job. Many self-development books point readers to the mind and to the adjustment of beliefs and perspectives. Those who have dedicated themselves to discovering the secrets of success and happiness sooner or later understand that life is first created from within. From there, fulfilling our potential is just a matter of aligning our beliefs and behaviors with our highest ideals.

The only things holding us back from the fulfillment we seek are ourselves and our own limiting beliefs. Thus, we are our only chance at the lives we desire. After all, we only have ourselves to hold accountable for our perspectives about our lives' conditions. Liberation is within our grasp though. As we remain patient with ourselves, we can encourage our supercomputer brains to work in our favor. And through practice, as our awareness increases, we can better apply our intellects for greater good. Like the great Hindu sage, Ramana Maharshi, once said, "Wanting to reform the world without discovering one's true self is like trying to cover the world with leather to avoid the pain of walking on stones and thorns. It is much simpler to wear shoes."

The Goals of Entrepreneurship

An individual making $200,000 per year but spending $210,000 isn't wealthy; neither is the individual who aimlessly hoards cash across several bank accounts while family and friends live without adequate comforts and necessities. The person working forty hours a week to make $120,000 a year isn't better off than the person spending fifteen hours a week to make $60,000 a year. In fact, the person working fifteen hours a week is at an advantage. He or she not only earns more per hour of working time but also has more free time and therefore more opportunities for growth—personal, professional, or otherwise. This is how financial education teaches us to be free in a capitalist system. (See chapter sixteen for more information about understanding money.)

This understanding of financial freedom is especially important for entrepreneurs. To be free within these systems is to know as much as possible about money—illusions and all. Successful entrepreneurs know the ways to earn money, manage it, increase it, and, most importantly, to spend it. Just as successful entrepreneurs learn to identify what wealth actually means to them, they also learn to distinguish assets from liabilities. They pay significant attention to the opportunity costs of all their decisions.

The goal of successful entrepreneurs isn't necessarily to have more personal gains but to increase prosperity and freedom for themselves and for all others they work with. With a thorough understanding of the marketplace, and with their goals in mind, the greatest entrepreneurs start out working for little to no profit. Instead, they find ways to exchange value through products or services for the money they need to create the changes they desire. Then they scale and automate, creating a small business and an independent income stream. By leveraging technology and systems to benefit them, entrepreneurs adopt a more expansive perspective of what a business truly is: a network of united but individual patterns, each contributing to a larger pattern that produces a specific desired result.

Entrepreneurs have automated systems in place that allow transactions, cash flow, and growth to happen without requiring the entrepreneurs' real-time presence. They don't trade their time for money; they create systems that actively solve problems and can continue to work for them over time. This is how entrepreneurs earn money while they sleep.

Entrepreneurs who have effectively created these limitless machines work harder on themselves than on any job or task because they've learned that perspective and mindset are the keys to achievement. Rather than having doubts about the future or hoping for the best, entrepreneurs apply their beliefs and focus their study and imagination to overcome their negative self-talk. Instead of viewing a business as a place to work and earn money, they see it as a thing to cultivate—an organized set of operations that produces solutions for people's problems, which then results in profits. Their actual objective isn't just to grow their businesses, but to build financial confidence.

With an established understanding of business development, marketing, accounting, and law, successful entrepreneurs work *on* their businesses, not just *in* them. They train themselves to separate themselves from their business in order to see what needs to be done. Recognizing who their customers are (marketing), they know exactly how to be of service (innovation). At the root level, master entrepreneurs understand that it's not about the company, product, or service; it's about the customer receiving more value from their efforts than from anywhere else.

Our work and our business ventures are merely reflections of our inner selves. Successful entrepreneurs understand this and don't view their work as punishment. Rather, they view their labor as opportunities to see themselves as they truly are: practitioners and creators of their lives' circumstances.

Self-aware entrepreneurs recognize that how we do one thing is how we do everything. Therefore, when these entrepreneurs come to work, their attention is on the work. They're present with what needs to be done, and consequently they perform the best that they can in the given circumstances. In this sense, they view the business as a vehicle to navigate through the marketplace, through their dojo.

Thus, entrepreneurship is a door to self-awareness.

Success is as dangerous as failure. Hope is as hallow as fear.

What does it mean that success is as dangerous as failure? Whether you go up the ladder or down it, your position is shaky. When you stand with your two feet on the ground, you will always keep your balance.

What does it mean that hope is as hallow as fear? Hope and fear are both phantoms that arise from thinking of the self. When we don't see the self as self, what do we have to fear?

See the world as your self. Have faith in the way things are. Love the world as your self; then you can care for all things.

—Tao Te Ching, *Lao Tzu, verse 13*

Urgency promotes decisiveness, and decisions lead to action.

18 MINDING WHAT MATTERS

A martial arts student went to his teacher and said earnestly, "I am devoted to studying your martial system. How long will it take me to master it?"

The teacher's reply was casual: "Ten years."

Impatiently, the student answered, "But I want to master it faster than that. I will work very hard. I will practice every day, ten or more hours a day if I must. How long will it take then?"

The teacher thought for a moment. "Twenty years."[92]

The Lack of Time

One hundred and fifty years from now, everyone who is walking this planet right now will very likely be dead.

Our fleeting existence in these bags of flesh is just as real as the birth of a new life. We carry the idea that we're *living* life, but because human consciousness can only distinguish by contrast; therefore, it's just as accurate to say we're *dying*. Our bodies and everything around them are in a constant state of decay. Every second that goes by, we inch closer to our inevitable demise.

This might seem like a grim start to the end of the book, but it's to serve a purpose (*memento mori*). That purpose has to do with

the fundamental yearning for growth within all living organisms. Humans especially feel this longing. When life and its experiences have been stagnant for too long, that deep-rooted desire to create change awakens; and change is a prerequisite for growth.

The purpose behind the sobering reminders is urgency and focusing on what matters—which happen to be the two factors (urgency and focus) that promote the neurochemicals that trigger neuroplasticity.[93] As Jack Kornfield said in *Buddha's Little Instruction Book*, "The trouble is, you think you have time."[94]

Everyone deals with procrastination at one point or another. Some learn to overcome it early; most cope with it over the course of their entire lives. If we play the observer of ourselves and sincerely reflect on our moments of procrastination, we'll notice the root cause to our stalling behavior: pain that we associate with performing a given task.

When we're procrastinating, if a task is important to us and has a deadline, we'll likely complete it; we'll just wait until the last minute so that we can avoid the pain of doing it as long as possible. As we approach the deadline, the pain of *not* doing it becomes higher than the pain of doing it, and it's at that moment that we suddenly become laser focused, leaping into action.

It's like when we wake up late for work because we slept through the alarm. We scramble to get out of bed to get ready and get to work on time. There's no time to relax in the warm, cozy bed; our job and income are on the line. The pain and discomfort of cold are no match.

Urgency promotes decisiveness, and decisions lead to action. This pattern is even evident in sales strategies with limited-time offers. We don't really care that something is 40% off, but as soon as we think we won't be able to get it later at 40% off, we're forced to decide *now*. And the fear of missing out pressures us into taking advantage of the sale while we still can.

What approach is better for motivating ourselves to do the things we want to do, to become the people we want to be, than the knowledge that we're not guaranteed an opportunity to do it later?

Reflecting on our vision for life, and on the end of life, can be a powerful conductor for the energy needed to make necessary changes. Think about how you would live your life if you knew you only had one week to live. How would you behave toward others? What would you do during your time alone? What would really be important to you?

We came into this life pure and screaming for adventure. In childhood we were filled with joy and the world was our playground. As we grew older, we were supposed to learn to see even more wonder in the world. But these days are different. Do we really want to leave our lives in the conditions they're currently in?

The Ability to Change

Before this age, accessing information to help us solve our problems was incredibly difficult. Now, with the global mind we've created called the internet, we're able to access information and learn at a tremendous rate. Mankind has been building and striving toward this day of technological advancements for thousands of years. We are experiencing our evolution this very day. Yet, many don't see this profound fact unfolding right before their eyes.

Previously the curious seekers had to travel substantial distances and wait long periods of time for new teachings, books, or scriptures, often risking their lives in the process. But in our world today we have tools that are changing our reality instantaneously. Right now we have an overwhelming possibility for communication that reaches across time and space. Distance doesn't matter anymore because billions of us are linked together. Technology has given us the creative capacity to fundamentally change humanity and truly overcome our limits. We've designed incredible devices that have radically redefined our boundaries and what it means to be human. This is without a doubt the most incredible era to be experiencing within recorded history.

This is the time to understand more about ourselves. Now that we're more closely connected to one another than ever before, we have the power to create tremendous changes in society today. We are at the forefront of completely transforming our civilization for generations to come.

Truly, human life is precious. There's an infinite amount of possibilities within each of us. It doesn't take any special education to recognize that being born a human on this planet has massive advantages. Each one of us has incredible latent powers that can increase the quality of not only our own lives but everyone else's as well. We tap into these powers when we take control of our energies and discipline ourselves to do what we know in our hearts we must do.

Our capacity for inner transformation relates to our education and conditioning, which are both things within our influence and control. The ego—the people we think we are—is merely an attachment to the thoughts, feelings, and behaviors of our pasts. In other words, an incomplete idea of ourselves is driving the momentum of our habits and experience of life. If we can make enduring changes to our behaviors, we can change our awareness and our ideas of ourselves (the self-image). Likewise, when we can shed the layers of our self-image, we can change our behaviors.

We can categorize the basic stages that bring us to make changes in attitude and behavior. These phases of development are apparent across changes in any branch of life, whether in our personal, professional and financial, family, or social lives. The stages are (1) learning, (2) creating conviction, and (3) effective action.

Learning

We know we need change when the information and behaviors we've been putting into practice begin to fail us. Therefore, the first step to creating any change is to find better information and absorb as much of it as possible. Once we know what we want and we've decided on what type of information will bring the best change, we can then search for quality material from reliable sources. Thankfully, in this age of information we can easily learn from what other people have done and are doing. What we do is experiment and imitate, then we collect data so that we can innovate. Our goal should never be to completely mimic. We should just try to learn what's useful and then develop our own individual style. For example, a rookie mixed martial arts fighter can imitate the boxing combinations his coach shows him, but if he never applies what he's learned in his own unique way, he'll never exercise his creativity to reach his potential. He can throw his hand at his opponent, or he can engage the floor with his back foot to generate force to propel energy up his body through his hips and out his arm onto his target. He can flow with genuine self-expression or he can repeat movements like an inflexible robot. The difference is the inner realization of what is *happening* through the individual, rather than what the individual is *doing*. What separates these two forms of action is self-awareness.

The proper use of knowledge is application through wholesome actions. There will always be some information to regard and some to discard; as Bruce Lee said, "Absorb what is useful, reject what is useless, add what is essentially your own."[95]

Familiarizing ourselves with the pattern of how we learn can be more important than any skill or amount of talent. In the stage of learning we feed information to our supercomputer brain for evaluation. As information compounds, we create patterns within our minds and increase our understanding with newfound data, we become more cognizant of what takes us closer to our desired changes and what takes us further away. With newformed perspectives, we adjust our beliefs and modify our values and, consequently, our priorities. These altered priorities then change our approach to life because we now know more and believe and want differently. And since our willingness to *do* arises from a firm belief that we *can* do, conviction will eventually make all changes possible—no matter how many attempts it takes.

Learning with the intention to adjust our ideas and to create an alternative view of what's possible—a new belief within ourselves— is the first step to change.

Creating Conviction

Once we've exposed ourselves to the right information, turned it into personalized knowledge, and gained understanding about what's possible for us, we can then reinforce our resolve by creating conviction.

Intention is a powerful driving force. Knowing why we're doing what we're doing is the power behind our determination. It's the reason we push through the tough times. When we're feeling good, it's easy to be where we need to be and do what we need to do. The trouble comes when we're feeling off. Who wants to show up at their worst? Having a strong enough reason for wanting something will give us the strength to crush inner resistance and halt all negotiations with the self. Most importantly, though, it will give us a reason to get back up when we fall. And if we're pursuing anything worthwhile, we *will* fall.

Pain is guaranteed in life, but for the most part, we can choose the pain we want to endure rather than letting the pain choose us.

For instance, we can choose the pain of discipline, or we can be forced to endure the pain of regret. Constantly making the easy decisions will lead to a hard life. However, disciplining the mind so that it makes what society has labeled *the hard decisions* will lead to an easier life. Once one aligns themselves internally as the type of person that makes those hard decisions, the behavior flows naturally.

Each of us has imagined a blueprint of how we think life should be and how we should act. If our lives aren't matching those blueprints, and we don't see ourselves making progress toward our desires, we're likely to feel unsatisfied with ourselves. A strong enough reason to change—or, rather, an honest enough reason to change—will help us bridge the gap between where we are and where we want to be. The greater the conviction about our growth, the more effort we'll be willing to invest—the more action we'll take. The more effort we invest, the more likely we are to notice progress. The more progress we notice, the more possibilities that open in our mind. And the more possibilities in our horizon, the stronger the conviction in our potential to create the circumstances we want. Continuous effort in the direction of our desire—showing up for ourselves and building upon previously created momentum—serves as the antidote to dissatisfaction.

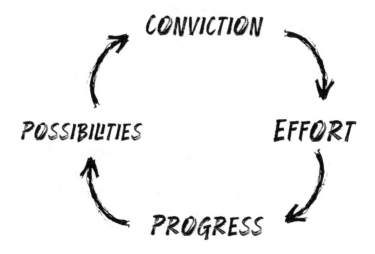

Effort is especially important when we're facing adversity. The human organism is built to not only handle failure but to learn from it. Unfortunately, through our conditioning, we forget how to cope with the letdowns. When we were in our purest states as babies, we had no problem failing. No one ever reported a baby give up on learning how to walk. None of us fell and stayed on the floor thinking, "This thing they're calling *walking* just isn't for me." Instead, we naturally persevered. Through constant effort, we put one foot in front of the other, making fewer mistakes each time. We eventually trained our brains to make a practice out of it. And ultimately, we were successful.

It's not the intelligent or the strong who survive as much as it is the adaptable. Those of us who become attached to our failures become stuck with certain limitations and eventually become rigid. And rigidity is a sign of weak conviction—and also of death.

Thankfully, we're designed to learn and adapt. We can gradually make our way back from even the lowest of conditions. By developing realistic expectations and adopting long-term views, we protect ourselves from paralyzing disappointment. Understanding that on some level we are imperfect beings who are likely to get stuck in our own ways, we must learn to be flexible in our thinking—to adapt to our circumstances. We taught ourselves to be the way we currently are; we can teach ourselves to be different.

In our hearts we know that there aren't any quick fixes. No hacks or magic formulas. Just slow growth through determination and effort—time and maturity. It's the steady effort in a single direction that eventually creates change.

Effective Action

The Japanese term *kaizen* translates to "change for the better" or "continuous improvement." The *kaizen* approach to creating change is especially noteworthy because it considers our emotional natures. Often when we have big goals, we can overwhelm ourselves into inaction. Likewise, when our expectations are too high, we can lose motivation to invest further effort because we don't see the progress we're expecting. The grand hopes we have might seem so out of reach that they don't seem achievable in this lifetime. Other times, our goals might be too small, and we don't believe it's worth expending the energy of effort—we don't believe it will create progress. By applying the *kaizen* method, we can overcome the quick-fix mentality and readjust ourselves to the mundane but time-tested and steady ways to improve.

We can apply the *kaizen* method by breaking our big goals into smaller goals that we know we can accomplish. Once the smaller goals are established as a plan in our minds, it's easier to take the necessary bite-size steps toward improving ourselves and accomplishing our bigger goals.

Kaizen is quite simple in application. It boils down to using small and simple actions to continuously become 0.01% better each day. Instead of trying to tackle a goal of fifty pushups when we know we can only do ten right now, we can modify our plan to just do what we can today. Then we can do slightly better tomorrow. The idea is to do as many small things as we can that will, day by day, move us toward our goals. The continual effort and minor advances accumulate, and over time we notice significant changes and improvements, particularly in our habits. Even the smallest step forward leads us further down our path. By staying persistent in our efforts, we eventually build the momentum necessary to not only reach our goals, but to surpass them as well.

It's important to note, especially for those who can be quickly discouraged, that although achieving our goals can be important, some goals aren't always meant to be reached. What's more important is that the changes in our behaviors enhance our skills and abilities and align our values and beliefs—our self-image. For example, we can fail at reaching our goal of one hundred pushups but can end up programming ourselves to be the type of person that exercises daily—a strong and healthy person. So the process of developing our visions or pursuing our goals is merely a process that, if we allow it, can turn us into the people we need—and want—to be. By putting our fears behind us as fuel and leveraging the force of habit to our advantage, we open the door to the possibility of achieving a goal without constant force of will. This is the process of aligning our nature to our vision.

Having a clear idea of what we want, with a solid, emotion-triggering reason for why we want it, will help us uncover the information and steps needed to make our desires a reality. When we use our imaginations to give emotional meaning to our undertakings, we set ourselves up for intuitive, effective action. This inevitably leads us to produce some result that in turn increases the possibilities we see within ourselves and, ultimately, the conviction we have about our growth.

Having this reinforced conviction is important because if we don't believe that progress can be made, it would be difficult to find a reason to make any attempts. This unwillingness to even try generally comes from emotional attachment to past failed attempts, meaning we're stuck reliving past experiences—stuck to certain ideas of ourselves. But, as we discussed in chapter four, we are not our past, nor are we limited within the confines of our self-images. We're ever-evolving, ever-experiencing, and ever-changing beings, far bigger, better, and capable of so much more than we think we are.

When people are driven by purpose and internal values, and they remain resilient in the face of adversity, very little can stop them from reaching what they set out for. Such people have conquered their reactions to the fear of hardship, discomfort, and the unknown. They are now comfortable walking into difficult situations because they've built up their courage like a muscle. Day by day, they confront their worries and anxieties and overcome obstacles. Often unknowingly, they gracefully bring to fruition the visions held in their minds.

By acting upon the guidance of the heart in coherence with the brain (as referenced in chapter thirteen), we remain centered in the moment, better able to adapt and move closer to satisfying our innate desires for growth and fulfillment. Our time may be limited, but impatience only makes us get in our own way. Exerting the right effort at the wrong time will make it the wrong effort. This is how a task can end up taking double or more the typically required time to complete—like in the case of the martial arts student in the beginning of this chapter. In other words, the more we rush a certain process, the more we run the risk of disharmonizing it. And if the process is out of harmony, the outcomes can turn out different than expected.

It's like when a wrestler steps in for a double leg takedown with too much distance between himself and his opponent. When the wrestler goes too early like this, the opponent will see the attempt, sprawl, and probably circle around to take the wrestler's back. The wrestler could have executed the technique of a double leg take-down flawlessly, but the fact that the wrestler didn't wait for the right time—when the opponent was within distance—made the effort wrong.

The more a person wants to learn, the more they can find to learn. However, learning is not enough. It's by *living* what's learned that we begin to develop. For instance, we can learn all there is to learn about human anatomy, muscles, and workouts. However, unless we begin to apply the workouts and exert our muscles, our anatomy will never change. We can study swimming and watch swimming all we want, but until we get in the water and swim, we're not swimming. With that in mind, we can't rush what will only come naturally. Our bodies will not be built, toned, and muscular after one or two intense workouts. It's not the individual workouts themselves that are important, nor is it the intensity of the workouts. The importance is in consistency and patience—and patience has everything to do with the act of letting go and allowing things to happen.

"We are all failures—at least, the best of us are." —James Matthew Barrie

"We are human beings living life within the human family, and we are exactly where we need to be right now.

CONCLUSION:
ALIGNING OURSELVES

In closing, it's important to crystalize the idea that although pain is natural, suffering is produced by irrational beliefs and distortions in thinking—our perspectives of ourselves, our circumstances, and our environments. Just as we have innate physical requirements like food, water, shelter, and clean air, we also have innate psychological requirements: to feel like we belong, to feel like we're worthy, to feel like our lives have meaning and purpose, and to feel like there are things to look forward to. To successfully live a human life is to be adaptable—to continuously refine our views. Having in mind our conditioned and limited nature, and the many ways we can become rigid in our thinking, we must always try to look at life with new eyes. After all, there's always more happening in any given instance than we can be consciously aware of.

Life is boundless and filled with possibility, and we can learn to see it that way too. Considering that about ninety-five percent of our programmed behavior is in the subconscious—the part of ourselves that we're unaware of—we may find that the very things we label as *problems* or *annoyances* hold deep lessons for us when we reflect upon them. With a certain degree of self-awareness, which can be achieved through practices like reflection and meditation, we can notice the subconscious mind externalizing our internal struggles. This understanding points to the one underlying deepest metaphysical secret: although they appear to be different, perhaps at times opposites, the outside *goes with* the inside just as the inside *goes with* the outside. So, as the saying goes, it helps to learn to read between the lines, and in this case, between the lines of our own thoughts—because that's where clarity is gained.

Human beings are meaning-assigning organisms. Our super-computer brains automatically compile the data they receive from our environments through our senses, then compute the data to come up with some sort of meaning so that we can make sense of our experiences. That meaning can either work for us or work against us. For instance, think back to your childhood when you woke up in the middle of the night to see a strange figure in the dark. Drowsy, half-asleep, and still in bed, you were probably startled, at the least. But then you turned on the light and saw that the figure was a stuffed animal in the corner of the room. As soon as the light came on, the meaning behind the figure changed and the threat became unreal. You realized it was your imagination taking you on an unpleasant ride. That's most of our fear and anxiety today.

Increasing our levels of awareness helps us see that our imaginations continue to deceive us on the most subtle levels. As we notice and confront these false perceptions, our minds open and we break free from the structure of our past conditioning. This clears the way for us to freely develop our potential and meet our highest mental health need: self-actualization. Through this process of matura-tion, we become stronger internally through discipline and gentler externally by a pleasant sense of character. This inner-outer balance helps us walk the path of the "middle way" (as referenced in chapter thirteen), and it becomes our nature to avoid extremes. Having this balance also contributes to a flexible mind—one that is accepting of life's circumstances without much resistance. When emotions arise, they move through us, and then they settle. We're fully present, yet nonattached; there's nothing to resist because we're able to adapt.

Take smoking for example. Smokers who want to quit usually feel that smoking is inherently bad and that they shouldn't be doing it. They are filled with resistance and spend loads of energy fight-ing the urges. But what would happen if their perspective on the smoking habit changed? What if they understood the impact smoking had on the human organism but didn't view it as something to be ashamed of? If it wasn't something to be ashamed of, they'd probably stop judging themselves. That alone would be a load off their shoulders. Then if they could sit without a smoke long enough, they might realize the deeper meaning behind their urge to smoke. They might realize their perceived need to smoke is merely an escape from themselves—an escape from some unacknowledged emotion. Sooner or later it becomes clear to them that they've conditioned themselves to feel the need to smoke out of an urge to manage that emotion. However, with a certain degree of self-awareness, and exposure to some techniques, one realizes that there are other, more effective ways to manage emotions. Yet, it isn't until we're at ease with ourselves—when we aren't spending loads of energy fighting ourselves—that there's energy available to direct in these other directions. This is why accepting our circumstances for what they are, without judgement, is always the first step to creating any sort of change.

A person must be patient with themselves if they want to take back control of their circumstances. The mind wants to cooperate, but it needs to be met with gentleness to become compliant. Direct and forceful ways expend a great deal of energy and aren't always the most fruitful. That's why instead of taking the perspective of *working on* the mind, it helps to find ways to *work with* the mind.

Because we know the mind naturally likes to cooperate, we can *work with* the mind by making inquiries that benefit us. Typically, people direct their mental faculties in such ways as to work against themselves. For example, they use their memory to recall past mistakes and shortcomings. A simple yet effective switch that we can make immediately is to begin asking our brain to recall past successes, times where we were happy with ourselves. Whatever we ask the mind to remember, it will remember. The faculty of imagination works the same way. If you're faced with a problem to solve and you tell yourself that this problem cannot be solved, your mind will look for all the ways to confirm the reasons why it cannot be solved.

However, if you believe that a solution is possible and you tell your mind to think of ways it is likely to be solved, it ramps up your creative forces to find probable solutions. In this way, our mind is our greatest servant. The only thing that's required of us is to gently guide it.

Underlying our intentions and actions is always belief, but most of us carry beliefs from others that we've adopted as our own due to our past conditioning. That's why the typical person's mind takes the role of 'ruthless master' instead of 'faithful servant'. As we discussed in Chapter 16, statements can close the mind, but questions can open it up. Asking ourselves powerful questions that challenge our beliefs is one surefire way to uncover aspects of our views that limit us. Some of the simplest yet profound ones for example are: "What am I a part of?" "Who am I really?" "What does this mean to me?" "What's most important to me?" "What do I need to improve?" "What do I need to do differently?".

The more we understand ourselves, the more we come to realize how we're constantly defining ourselves with limiting concepts. If we're honest with ourselves, we'll come to realize how we're imprisoning ourselves in our own minds. Therefore, creating a life of self-sufficiency involves exposing those limitations and shifting the idea we have of ourselves into something more limitless. Who and what we identify as will determine our behavior. Having an identity that is linked to the entire cosmos empowers us and positions our thinking in such a way that our life decisions naturally contribute to humanity and its evolution. What stands in the way of this mindset is our small self, our ego—our attachments to past experiences, our *idea* of who and what we are.

If we can learn to look past our idea of our self and restore our connection to our body's natural intelligence, we can begin to tap into deeper realms of intuition and, ultimately, meaningfully propel ourselves into a state of growth. The body already knows how to achieve self-sufficiency. Think of all the cells in your body working around the clock, without any direction from you, to sustain this organism. Growth happens naturally; mostly, it's our ideas that hinder the process. The person who wants to develop themselves in a sincere way must resist completely identifying with the egoic thinking mind and instead get into the feeling mind—the heart. That's where understanding and healing takes place.

With our minds and hearts harmonized, bringing together reason and intuition, we're grounded and centered with access to deep reservoirs of insight. With this kind of balance accompanied with a purpose in mind, one is not only better capable of withstanding life's challenges, but better able to mold those challenges into benefits that can drive them forward in their development, towards further opportunities.

Humans are naturally goal-striving beings. They function best when oriented toward desirable goals that they believe will positively affect their circumstances. Life is not just about the crucial case of surviving and achieving though. It's more like a sincere—but not so serious—wrestling match. When we grab on too tightly, we eventually get flipped over and pinned. However, by surrendering to what *is* and adapting accordingly, we have a better chance of gaining our desired position. This involves a commitment to go through the process without clinging to any part of it; it also demands the courage to remain in the present moment so that we can spot the opportunities as they arise. Anyone who's seen a master in the discipline of judo counter an opponent's perfectly executed throw has seen this principle in action.

The Taoists have a principle of being absent as a condition of being present. Chuang Tzu, the Chinese philosopher credited with writing one of the foundational texts on Taoism, once said, "You forget your feet when the shoes are comfortable. You forget your waist when the belt is comfortable."[96] When our clothes fit properly, they keep us warm but it's almost as if we aren't wearing any. On the other hand, if the clothes don't fit appropriately, they become a nuisance and we can't help but feel them. The application of this idea in our daily lives is to conduct ourselves in the world as if we're absent to it. This means that our mind doesn't get in our own way. We're free of judgements and without concern with what's happening. We're not for a particular situation, nor are we against it. Because our mind is perfectly simple, it sees no obstacle in its way. It behaves just as a mirror would: it refuses nothing, *holds* whatever it sees but doesn't *keep* it. In this way, one is completely detached and has no regrets for the past, nor anxieties of the future. Instead, they move in accordance with nature, for in truth neither past nor future have any existence outside the eternal Now.

We are human beings living life within the human family, and we're exactly where we need to be right now. We may at times think we're out of harmony with life, but we can't be. Life is an unfolding of the present moment, and here you are, now. You can't escape this moment, nor can you catch it by trying. The urge we feel within to grow is simply a call to consciously participate in this unfoldment. It's a call to inner discipline and self-actualization—the innate psychological need that helps us become closer to all that this organism can be before its time here is up.

Inner discipline is the true meaning behind a spiritual life. It's the *way* of the warrior's spirit.

Practicing inner discipline trains our psychological and emotional states to improve our wellbeing; it helps us become compassionate and patient as we continually struggle to understand and, as Carl Jung expressed, *integrate* the darkness within each of us. As we familiarize ourselves with our darker half, we see ourselves more clearly. We become grounded and whole and we accept ourselves as a more complete being. In doing so, it becomes easier to accept others—with their own darkness and all.

This is how we humans adapt and shape life's circumstances to give us what we so deeply desire: a full and overall enjoyable experience of life.

Within each of us remains the ability to choose what experiences mean to us, where we put our attention, and how we will approach the unfoldment of life—and ultimately, death.

These choices will determine the course of our experience of life. They'll determine how freely our spirit expresses itself. And they'll determine our ability to self-realize.

This is the essence of aligning ourselves for the freedom we all seek.

This is *Wired for Success*.

NOTES

1. Lydy Walker, "#120 Letter to Pearl," *BruceLee.com*, October 17, 2018.

2. Nyogen Senzaki and Paul Reps, *Zen Flesh, Zen Bones: A Collection of Zen and Pre-Zen Writings*, Tuttle Publishing, 1998, p. 23.

3. *Enter the Dragon*, Warner Bros. Pictures, 1973.

4. Jen Atalla, Jessica Orwig, and Lamar Salter, "A Neuroscientist Explains Why Reality May Just Be a Hallucination," *BusinessInsider.com*, March 26, 2018.

5. Megan Leonhardt, "Americans Spend over $1,000 a Year on Lotto Tickets," *CNBC.com*, December 12, 2019.

6. Sabrina Ricci, "Guest Post: How Much Do Americans Spend on Books?" *DigitalPubbing.com*, April 22, 2020.

7. Melissa Dahl, "A Classic Psychology Study on Why Winning the Lottery Won't Make You Happier," *TheCut.com*, January 13, 2016.

8. Franklin Kirk, "2 twin boys were raised by an alcoholic father," *Facebook.com*, January 15, 2013.

9. *The Matrix*, Warner Bros. Pictures, 1999.

10. Alan Watts, "1.1.1.—Not What Should Be—Pt. 1," *AlanWatts.org*, April 16, 2019.

11. Niklas Göke, "Zen Stories for a Calm, Clear & Open Mind," *Medium.com*, July 22, 2019.

12. Alan Watts, "1.1.4.—Coincidence of Opposites," *AlanWatts.org*, April 16, 2019.

13. Alan Watts, "'Do You Do It Or Does It Do You?' by Alan Watts (Complete Lecture and Transcript)," *Organism.Earth*, n.d.

14. Victoria Rideout and Michael B. Robb, "Social Media, Social Life: Teens Reveal Their Experiences," *CommonSenseMedia.org*, 2018.

15. Deidre McPhillips, "U.S. Among Most Depressed Countries in the World," *USNews.com*, September 14, 2016.

16. Joseph H. Arguinchona and Prasanna Tadi, "Neuroanatomy, Reticular Activating System," *NCBI.NLM.NIH.gov*, July 31, 2020.

17. Margaret Semrud-Clikeman, "Research in Brain Function and Learning," *APA.org*, 2010.

18. Matt Valentine, "Right and Wrong, ...Zen," *KindSpring.org*, May 16, 2018.

19. "Human Brain Loves Surprises, Research Reveals," *ScienceDaily.com*, April 16, 2001.

20. Maxwell Maltz, *Psycho-Cybernetics*, Los Angeles: TarcherPerigee, 2015, p. 22.

21. Mark, "Elephant and the Chain," *PossibleMind.co.uk*, November 20, 2012.

22. Alan Watts, "Creating Who You Are," *ThirdMonk.net*, n.d..

23. "Moving Mind," *Users.Rider.edu*, 1997.

24. "The History of Tobacco Marketing: It's a Scary Story," *StopsWithMe.com*, 2020.

25. National Academy of Sciences, "Tobacco Advertising and Promotion," *NCBI.NLM.NIH.gov*, 1994.

26. The Associated Press, "Disney to Buy Pixar for $7.4 Billion," *NYTimes.com*, January 24, 2006.

27. Wikipedia contributors, "Abraham Maslow," *Wikipedia.org*, December 11, 2020.

28. "'You've Got to Find What You Love,' Jobs Says," *News.Stanford.com*, June 14, 2005.

29. Niklas Göke, "Zen Stories for a Calm, Clear & Open Mind," *Medium.com*, January 10, 2019.

30. Romeo Vitelli, "Can You Change Your Personality?" *PsychologyToday.org*, September 7, 2015.

31. Marianne Szegedy-Maszak, "Mysteries of the Mind: Your Unconscious Is Making Your Everyday Decisions," *Faculty.FortLewis.edu*, February 28, 2005.

32. Britta K. Hölzel et al., "Mindfulness Practice Leads to Increases in Regional Brain Gray Matter Density," *Psychiatry Research*, 191, no. 1 (November 20, 2010): 36–43.

33. "'You've Got to Find What You Love,' Jobs Says," *News.Stanford.com*, June 14, 2005.

34. Shunryū Suzuki, "Zen Mind, Beginner's Mind," *DailyZen.com*, 1970, p. 10.

35. John Heider, *Tao of Leadership*, Green Dragon Publishing Group, 1722, p. 18.

36. Trent T. Gilliss, "The Little Monk and the Samurai: A Zen Parable," *OnBeing.org*, May 14, 2013.

37. Jasper Bergink, "Determining the World's Happiness Map: From 'Mutluluk' to 'Shiawase,'" *ForAStateofHappiness.com*, March 6, 2018.

38. Matt. 4:4 (KJV).

39. "The Nature of Things," *TrueCenterPublishing.com*, n.d.

40. Dacher Keltner, "The Compassionate Instinct," *GreaterGood.Berkeley.edu*, March 1, 2004.

41. "The Biological and Emotional Causes of Aggression," *OpenTextBC.ca*, n.d.

42. Adams et al., "The Seville Statement on Violence," *Culture-of-Peace.info*, 2011.

43. Brandon H. Hidaka, "Depression as a Disease of Modernity: Explanations for Increasing Prevalence," *NCBI.NLM.NIH.gov*, January 12, 2012.

44. Christian Keysers and Valeria Gazzola, "Hebbian Learning and Predictive Mirror Neurons for Actions, Sensations And Emotions," *NCBI.NLM.NIH.gov*, June 5, 2014.

45. Dalai Lama X. I. V., *Mind in Comfort and Ease*, Boston: Wisdom Publications, 2007, p. 17.

46. "ZEN STORY: 'The Horse' (Mindfulness)," *AmiraCarluccio.com*, August 31, 2016.

47. Brian Tracy, "Subconscious Mind Power Explained," *BrianTracy.com*, n.d.

48. Kayla Matthews, "Why We Should Look Forward to More of Each Day," *TinyBuddha.com*, 2019.

49. Jim Davies, "Most of the Mind Can't Tell Fact from Fiction," *Nautil.us*, September 22, 2019.

50. Marianne Szegedy-Maszak, "Mysteries of the Mind," *Webhome .Auburn.edu*, n.d.

51. Rollo May, *Man's Search for Himself*, W. W. Norton & Company, 2009, p. 159.

52. Annie Murphy Paul, "Your Brain on Fiction," *NYTimes.com*, March 17, 2012.

53. Lidija Globokar, "The Power of Visualization and How to Use It," *Forbes.com*, March 4, 2020.

54. Mark 11:24 (KJV).

55. Wikipedia contributors, "Shadow (Psychology)," *Wikipedia.org*, November 5, 2020.

56. Wikipedia contributors, "Psychological Projection," *Wikipedia.org*, December 7, 2020.

57. James Allen, *As a Man Thinketh*, New York: Simon & Schuster, 1903, pp. 13–14.

58. Noah Rasheta, "The Truth of Unsatisfactoriness," *SecularBuddhism. com*, accessed July 15, 2021, *secularbuddhism.com/131-the-truth-of-unsatis-factoriness/*.

59. "#11 Walk On," *BruceLee.com*, accessed July 15, 2021, brucelee .com/podcast-blog/2016/9/21/11-walk-on.

60. J. D. Bremner, "Traumatic Stress: Effects on the Brain," *Dialogues in Clinical Neuroscience*, vol. 8, no. 4, 2006, pp. 445–461, doi:10.31887/DCNS .2006.8.4/jbremner.

61. "How Unprocessed Trauma Is Stored in the Body," *Coalition Recovery*, accessed February 16, 2021, coalitionrecovery.com/rehab-blog/ how-unprocessed-trauma-is-stored-in-the-body/.

62. Jonathan E. Sherin and Charles B. Nemeroff, "Post-Traumatic Stress Disorder: The Neurobiological Impact of Psychological Trauma," *Dialogues in Clinical Neuroscience*, vol. 13, no. 3, 2011, pp. 263–78, doi:10.31887 /DCNS.2011.13.2/jsherin.

63. Rob Waters, "Addiction Rooted In Childhood Trauma, Says Prominent Specialist," *California Healthline*, accessed July 16, 2021, californiahealthline.org/news/addiction-rooted-in-childhood-trauma-says-prominent-specialist/.

64. Jim Rendon, "How Trauma Can Change You—for the Better," *Time*, accessed July 17, 2021, time.com/3967885/how-trauma-can-change-you-for-the-better/.

65. R. G. Tedeschi and L. G. Calhoun, "The Posttraumatic Growth Inventory: Measuring the Positive Legacy of Trauma," *J Trauma Stress*, vol. 9, no. 3 (July 1996): 455–71, doi:10.1007/BF02103658, PMID: 8827649.

66. G. T. Doran, "There's a S.M.A.R.T. Way to Write Management's Goals and Objectives," *Management Review*, vol. 70, no. 11 (1981): 35–36.

67. David Chadwick, "Spiritual Quotation," *SpiritualityandPractice .com*, n.d.

68. John Henry Newman, "Chapter 1. One the Development of Ideas," *NewmanReader.org*, 2007.

69. Lachlan Brown, "The Real Meaning of Buddhist Detachment & Why Most of Us Get it Wrong," *HackSpirit.com*, May 7, 2020.

70. Dalai Lama X. I. V., *Ethics for the New Millennium*, New York: Riverhead Books, 2001, p. 56.

71. Leon C. Megginson, "Lessons from Europe for American Business," *The Southwestern Social Science Quarterly*, vol. 44, no. 1 (1963): 3–13.

72. Rory Stirling, "The Rabbi and the Lobster," *Medium.com*, August 11, 2017.

73. Olga Khazan, "Can Three Words Turn Anxiety Into Success?" *TheAtlantic.com*, March 23, 2016.

74. Wikipedia contributors, "Three Poisons," *Wikipedia.org*, October 7, 2020.

75. "Evil and Suffering," *BBC.co.uk*, 2020.

76. "Alan Watts: The Story of the Chinese Farmer," *WellsBaum.blog*, January 27, 2008.

77. "Take Care of Yourself First, Then Others," *HilaryFraser.com*, November 9, 2017.

78. Jessica Stoller-Conrad, "Microbes Help Produce Serotonin in Gut," *Caltech.edu*, April 9, 2015.

79. Giuseppe Danilo Vighi et al., "Allergy and the Gastrointestinal System," *NCBI.NLM.NIH.gov*, September 2008.

80. "Energetic Communication," *HeartMath.org*, 2020.

81. "Heart-Brain Communication," *HeartMath.org*, 2020.

82. K. Sri Dhammananda Maha Thera, "The Noble Eightfold Path—The Middle Way," *BudSas.org*, n.d.

83. "The Two Travelers and the Farmer," *Spellbinders.org*, 2020.

84. Francesca Perry, "Does City Life Make Us More or Less Lonely? Share Your Stories," *TheGuardian.com*, February 29, 2016.

85. Karyn Hall, "Accepting Loneliness," *PsychologyToday.com*, January 13, 2013.

86. Hara Estroff Marano, "What Is Solitude?" *PsychologyToday.com*, July 1, 2003.

87. Ruwan M. Jayatunge, "Joseph Stalin—Psychopathology of a Dictator," *ColomboTelegraph.com*, May 23, 2014.

88. Alan W. Watts, *The Book: On the Taboo against Knowing Who You Are*, Vintage Books, 1989, pp. 61.

89. Jim Clifton, "The World's Broken Workplace," *News.Gallup.com*, June 13, 2017.

90. Charles Eisenstein, *Sacred Economics: Money, Gift, and Society in the Age of Transition*, North Atlantic Books, 2011, p. 33.

91. Napoleon Hill, *Think and Grow Rich*, New York: Ballantine Books, 1983.

92. "Power in Patience," *DilipNaidu.Wordpress.com*, March 4, 2015.

93. "Joe Rogan Experience #1513 Andrew Huberman," Interview by MOTIVATOR, *YouTube.com*, November 27, 2020, video, 36:46.

94. Jack Kornfield, *Buddha's Little Instruction Book*, New York: Bantam, 1994.

95. "#63 Research Your Own Experience," *BruceLee.com*, 2020.

96. Burton Watson, trans., *The Complete Works of Chuang Tzu*, Columbia University Press, p. 165.

INDEX

About the Author

At twenty-one, Edmond Abramyan built a successful e-commerce and wholesale business, and within one year, he expanded into distribution with his own product line, which maintained profitability for over ten years. And he started all this with just $160. Today, Edmond is still in business, and he's also an author, investor, and consultant, as well as a mentor to newer entrepreneurs, helping them develop business strategies and mindsets so that they can grow their businesses online. To this end, he has spent years cultivating business and psychological acumen and is no stranger to starting different types of companies from the ground up. His idea is that a person's philosophy is the number one factor that holds them back from tapping into the creative genius within to solve everyday challenges.

You can learn more about Edmond and his work when you visit his website, edabramyan.com.